Ella Hickson

OIL

NICK HERN BOOKS

London

www.nickhernbooks.co.uk

A Nick Hern Book

Oil first published as a paperback original in Great Britain in 2016 by Nick Hern Books Limited, The Glasshouse, 49a Goldhawk Road, London W12 8QP

Oil copyright © 2016 Ella Hickson

Ella Hickson has asserted her right to be identified as the author of this work

Cover photograph by Miles Aldridge

Designed and typeset by Nick Hern Books, London
Printed in the UK by CPI Books (UK) Ltd

A CIP catalogue record for this book is available from the British Library

ISBN   978 1 84842 603 0

Oil was first performed at the Almeida Theatre, London, on 14 October 2016 (previews from 7 October). The cast was as follows:

MAY	Anne-Marie Duff
MR FAROUK	Nabil Elouahabi
THOMAS/MR THOMAS/TOM	Brian Ferguson
MA SINGER	Ellie Haddington
SAMUEL/OFFICER SAMUEL/SAMMY	Patrick Kennedy
AMY	Yolanda Kettle
JOSS	Tom Mothersdale
ANNE/ANA/AMINAH	Lara Sawalha
WILLIAM WHITCOMB/NATE	Sam Swann
FANNY/FAN WANG	Christina Tam

Direction	Carrie Cracknell
Design	Vicki Mortimer
Movement Direction	Joseph Alford
Lighting	Lucy Carter
Dramaturg	Jenny Worton
Composition	Stuart Earl
Sound	Peter Rice
Video	Luke Halls
Casting	Julia Horan CDG

Resident Direction	Taio Lawson
Costume Supervision	Claire Wardroper
Design Assistant	Matt Hellyer
Associate Lighting Designer	Max Narula
Sound Assistant	Harry Johnson
Video Associate	Alex Uragallo
Video Programmer	Dan Bond
Dialect	Kay Welch
Farsi Translations and Dialect	Haydeh Eftekhar
Arabic Translations and Dialect	Silvia El Helo
Mandarin Translations	Cennydd John
Pinyin Translations	Ruhua Hele
Mandarin Dialect	Jessica Dong

Acknowledgements

I would like to thank the NT Studio, The MacDowell Colony, Pentabus Theatre, Laura Diehl and the Goethe Institute Berlin, the RSC and The Upton Cressett Foundation for their generosity in providing the space and time to write. My thanks to Rachel Taylor for constantly good counsel.

I would like to thank Colin Campbell for the hours he spent sharing his work on Peak Oil with me and Richard Baker for putting us in touch. I'd like to thank my dad, Peter Hickson, for answering endless questions about the industry.

I'd like to thank Rupert Goold, Ben Power, Rob Icke, Ian Rickson and Sacha Wares for their input along the way. My thanks, especially, to Rupert for his longstanding and unflinching faith in me and in this project.

I would like to thank my friends and family for six years of encouragement and conversation, their support has been crucial in completing a project of this scale.

This play has benefitted hugely from the creative input of an incredible team and company. It has been a pleasure and privilege to work with you all.

My thanks to Jenny Worton and Carrie Cracknell for their intellectual rigour and compassion in the dramaturgical wrangling of this play. It's been a dream team.

Thank you, Crackers, for taking the solitude out of ambition. It has broadened the horizons of what is possible.

E.H.

For my family

'The urge to form partnerships, to link up in collaborative arrangements, is perhaps the oldest, strongest, and most fundamental force in Nature. There are no solitary, free-living creatures, every form of life is dependent on other forms.'

Lewis Thomas

'You cannot be a feminist and a capitalist – feminism is about freeing women from oppression, and capitalism oppresses all women.'

Ruth Wallsgrove

'...the first half of the age of oil now closes... it lasted 150 years and saw the rapid expansion of industry, transport, trade, agriculture and financial capital – allowing the population to expand six-fold. The second half now dawns, and will be marked by the decline of oil and all that depends on it; including financial capital.'

Colin Campbell

'Any sufficiently advanced technology is indistinguishable from magic.'

Arthur C. Clark

'My father rode a camel. I drive a car. My son flies a jet airplane. His son will ride a camel.'

A Saudi saying

Characters

MAY
AMY
JOSS
MA SINGER
ANNE/ANA/AMINAH
THOMAS/MR THOMAS/TOM
SAMUEL/OFFICER SAMUEL/SAMMY
FANNY/FAN WANG
WILLIAM WHITCOMB
NATE
MR FAROUK

Settings

Part One: 1889, Cornwall
Part Two: 1908, Tehran
Part Three: 1970, Hampstead
Part Four: 2021, Baghdad
Part Five: 2051, Cornwall

This text went to press before the end of rehearsals and so may differ slightly from the play as performed.

PART ONE

Farm, Cornwall – 1889

The Singer Family Farm: a remote smallholding in the West Country countryside.

Late afternoon, winter; it is bitingly cold, the snow is thick – the air is purple-grey.

A white sun is low in the sky. JOSS, *twenty-five – physical, bulky – is splitting logs with a long-axe.* MAY, *twenty – hardy, slim, muscular and three months pregnant.* MAY *is frozen, dirty and hungry.* MAY *watches* JOSS. MAY *waits for* JOSS *to take a break so she can speak.* JOSS *splits a log.* JOSS *splits a log.* JOSS *splits a log.* JOSS *doesn't take a break.*

MAY. Joss?

JOSS. Hm?

–

MAY. Joss?

JOSS *keeps splitting logs.*

–

Joss? Joss? Joss? Joss?

JOSS *raises the axe to strike again, as he does so* MAY *steps in towards it; the axe comes down centimetres from her face and lodges in the block.*

MAY *doesn't flinch.*

Pause.

It's not because I'm weak.

–

JOSS *crumples.*

JOSS. God's sake.

–

MAY. Sun's going down. (*Beat*.) Been up to my elbows in freeze since noon.

JOSS. Why?

MAY. Drinking trough's frozen; inches thick – had to chip at it.

JOSS. You get 'em all done?

MAY. Baby's making me tired; hungry as hell. Joss?

JOSS. You get 'em done?

MAY. All but two.

JOSS. They need doing or animals can't drink.

MAY. Can't feel my fingers.

JOSS. We can't have you in bed, not yet.

MAY. I can't feel my fingers.

JOSS. Rub 'em together.

–

MAY. Put your arms around me.

JOSS. If you get warm you'll be colder than you started five minutes after.

MAY. Then keep your arms around me.

JOSS. If I stop it'll be hell getting goin' again.

MAY. Please.

JOSS. Don't make it seem cruel, May – it's work.

JOSS *keeps splitting logs*.

–

MAY. I'll fetch some bread and cheese from the pantry, few logs and we can set up in here, I can sit with you whilst you work, I'll bring the chicken in for plucking and we can sit warm together.

MA SINGER *has entered unseen – tall, thin and beaky.*

MA SINGER. Not enough for all five up there to be making picnics down here for two, Joss.

JOSS. Mother.

MA SINGER. Thought you were clearing the troughs, May – far as I could see two still frozen over.

MAY. Ice was too thick.

MA SINGER. Half a dozen sheep gaspin'.

Pause.

MAY. I was just coming by to see if… Joss had wood for me.

–

MA SINGER. Find you in these stables lot more than I find you working.

MAY. I like the stables.

MA SINGER. Must be a natural instinct of sorts.

MAY. Dare say.

–

JOSS. Well now. May, go get warm up in the house and I'll do those troughs for you when I'm through here.

MAY. No, no – they'll be done. Then we'll have our picnic, Joss – just us.

MAY *kisses* JOSS*'s cheek.*

MAY *turns to leave.*

MA SINGER. May?

MAY *stops and turns back.*

Why is it that you think you should be warm when the sun ain't shining?

–

MAY *exits.*

JOSS *turns away and starts chopping logs again.*

MAY *sees him and turns to walk up to the house.*

The kitchen. Early evening. Winter.

Candles. Black walls.

FANNY *uses washing board and tub and scrubs vigorously at underclothes.*

MAY *tugs and plucks at a slightly rotten chicken.*

MA SINGER *is loading the range with more coal.*

ANNE *is hefting all the weight she has into kneading dough.*

MAY. Feathers ripping out more flesh than they should.

MA SINGER. It's fine.

MAY. Doesn't smell right.

MA SINGER. Smells fine.

MAY. It's.

FANNY. Not going to rot in this freeze, is it?

MA SINGER. Exactly.

ANNE *holds up the dough.*

MA SINGER *comes round – takes a piece of the dough – smooths it out in front of the candle – the light shines through it and shows that there are still lumps.*

Needs to look like parchment – not porridge. You see?

ANNE. Quicker to make parchment, I reckon. Hardly feel my arms.

MA SINGER. You're doing a good job.

FANNY. Range is smeeching; smoke's getting to these shirts.

MA SINGER. Do 'em outside.

MAY. It's pitch black.

MA SINGER. Need to get them done, don't we? Can't send those boys out in this weather with damp shirts.

MAY. It's not right, this chicken.

MA SINGER. Will you stop whining? Do these potatoes; I can't get my hands round them.

MAY *picks up the potatoes and reaches for a knife*. MA SINGER *starts in with the washing*.

Brush 'em don't cut 'em not enough as there is – we'll lose half to the pigs you go cutting them and clean all that up first – you never do a job properly you, do you?

ANNE *squeals*.

What you done, love?

ANNE. Piece a glass, I think. Pass that candle.

MAY *reaches for the candle to come and look*.

MA SINGER. You got work to do.

MA SINGER *takes the candle off* MAY.

MAY. Bind it or you'll bleed into the bread.

ANNE. It hurts.

MAY. Find the glass 'n' all.

MA SINGER. It's all right, love, give it here – let's look at it.

Cut's clean.

MA SINGER *binds the cut*.

MAY. Find the piece of glass.

ANNE *gets back to kneading*.

Don't much like the idea of that glass being on the inside.

MA SINGER. Maybe you can have cake instead?

MAY. I don't think there's any one of us that's got insides above glass cutting into them, have we?

MA SINGER. Fifty years I've been running this house it's a miracle no one died before you came along and educated us on how to live.

MAY. You going to feed your boys bread with glass in it?

No answer.

Done plucking.

MA SINGER. Gut it.

MAY *picks the bird up and puts it on the table – brings a cleaver down hard on its head. The smell is intense.*

Make good what's good. Throw what's not.

Footsteps can be heard in the hall – boots being taken off.

ANNE. It's Sam. He's back early.

MAY *goes to the cupboard – and takes out a bottle of Scotch and moves it – the hides it behind the range.*

MA SINGER. May.

ANNE. Don't.

MAY. Bottles don't break on their own.

SAMUEL *enters and goes straight for the cupboard. He finds it empty.*

SAMUEL. It fucking stinks in here.

ANNE. Warm your hands by the range.

FANNY. You look frozen through.

SAMUEL. It's cold out.

SAMUEL *checks another cupboard.*

Wife.

He kisses ANNE. *She's warm. He takes her warmth. He looks about the room.*

Mother?

MA SINGER. You get the feed in?

SAMUEL. All but the bottom field, stock aren't going in there anyway. Ground's too hard. We been moving things around in here, have we?

FANNY. Your hands look red.

SAMUEL. Gone past red, Fan. This one's gone all the way to black.

MA SINGER. Let me look.

SAMUEL (*to* ANNE). Pair of injured soldiers, eh? What do you do there?

MA SINGER. We patched her up right enough.

MAY. Bit a glass, broken bottle I think.

SAMUEL *turns on* MAY. *Goes in really close.*

SAMUEL. What you think a that finger then? You think I'm going to get to keep it?

MAY. If you're lucky.

MA SINGER. That's no joke.

SAMUEL. That fowl stinks.

MAY *slops the guts into a bowl.*

MA SINGER. Sit. I'll get you some tea. We can't have you one hand down. Work in the woodshed tomorrow.

SAMUEL *sits for his tea. Watches* MAY. MA SINGER *places the tea in front of him.*

FANNY. Sun, this morning – sneaking across – catching things, lick of God it looked. Makes you grateful to be alive.

SAMUEL. Land's long and dark out there now.

SAMUEL *stands and pushes his chair back hard – gets* MAY *in a corner.*

MA SINGER. Sam?

SAMUEL. Mother loves me and the other two haven't got the spine.

MAY. Don't know what you're talking about.

SAMUEL. Knackered I am. Nothing in me. Drained, May.

MAY. Want to sit down and have your tea, take a weight off.

MA SINGER. Samuel.

SAMUEL. Not slept one night this week sound of you and Joss rutting.

MAY. You're hurting my face.

ANNE (*weakly*). Stop it, Sam.

SAMUEL. My wife sobbing 'bout the one we lost whilst she has to listen to you two fucking the night away. Not nice that? Not good people is it?

MA SINGER. Samuel Singer, you let go of her and sit your arse down in that chair right now.

SAMUEL. I'd like a drink.

MAY. As I say – take a seat, have your tea. Rest of us is busy making a meal.

SAMUEL *brings his face in close – grunts at her, clicks an underbite, guttural.*

SAMUEL *spots the bottle by the range. Picks it up. Gets a glass. Sits down.*

SAMUEL. Care to join me?

MAY. Fine for now, thanks.

SAMUEL. Have a drink with your husband's brother?

MAY. I'm still working on the bird; I'll be covered in blood again in seconds.

MA SINGER. You've got mud all over your face. Get yourself washed.

MAY. Sam's pure mud.

SAMUEL. I been in the fields, May. Man's work. Women should be clean – not all mucky.

MA SINGER. Won't take two minutes and then we can forget the whole thing.

MAY. But /

MA SINGER. / Must you fight me on every corner?

MAY. Pass some water out that kettle, will you – Fan?

MA SINGER. Kettle's for cooking. We need it for the dinner or we'll all be late eating, use the trough outside.

MAY. It's frozen over outside.

MA SINGER. I cleared the trough.

SAMUEL. You shouldn't be doing that, Ma. Your age, you should have asked one of us to do it.

MA SINGER. You were all working elsewhere.

SAMUEL hooks ANNE into him and nuzzles his face in her side.

ANNE. I got to keep going till it looks like parchment.

SAMUEL. Go on girl; go on!

MAY heads for the door, she stumbles – ANNE catches her, no one else sees.

ANNE (*aside to MAY as best she can*). You all right?

MAY. Fine.

ANNE. Get some rest. Eh?

MAY. I said I'm fine.

MAY exits to the porch.

The porch: MAY steps out – she can still hear the kitchen through the wall. The area is small – she rests against the door and tries to breathe. JOSS arrives through the dark – he carries wood.

JOSS. Damp as hell this. Need it dry tonight or we'll be low tomorrow.

JOSS goes to walk past MAY into the house.

MAY. I can't breathe, Joss – I can't.

JOSS (*bends in, thinking it's physical*). You all right?
Everything all right with the /

MAY. / There's nothing just mine, not my face, or skin, or
clothes, ears or my mouth – eyes on me all the time, don't
own what's under my skin. Joss?

JOSS *backs off – he's heard it before.*

Keep finding tears on my face by surprise. I ran and I stood
right at the end of the bottom field and – I swear, I could still
feel someone's breath on the side of my neck, Joss? We
could go – with the baby – our own little family – just us –
somewhere. Joss?

JOSS *stands – can't look at her – can't go into the house.*

You're the only thing that's mine. You're the only thing
I chose.

MAY *stands, puts the palm of his hand over her face.*

The size of you. The smell of you.

*She brings his head to her – breathes in his hair. She puts
her hand into his trousers.*

JOSS. Not here – wait, shh – no, May /

*/ He can't not – he kisses her. He lifts her up, light as a
feather and holds her against the wall. She wraps her legs
around him. He buries his face in her neck. There's a strange
combination of desperation and relief in it – a strange sort of
peace, like – at last, she can catch her breath.*

Laughter from SAMUEL *comes through the door. Something
smashes. Shouting.* JOSS *pushes* MAY *hard against the wall.*

MA SINGER *enters the porch.* JOSS *doesn't see her.* MAY
*still hoisted against the wall, her husband between her legs,
holds* MA SINGER*'s eye for a beat.*

MA SINGER. Work to be done.

JOSS *drops* MAY *almost immediately.*

JOSS. Snow got into the woodshed.

MA SINGER. Dinner is ready.

> JOSS *enters the kitchen*.

> You forgot the pail.

> MA SINGER *hands* MAY *the pail*.

> Bring it indoors.

MAY. I'm not washing in front of everyone.

MA SINGER. You'll catch your death out here.

MAY. Then I'll not wash.

MA SINGER. You'll wash yourself before sitting at my table.

> MA SINGER *goes back inside*.

> MAY *dips the pail into the icy water – she gasps*.

> MAY *exits through to the kitchen*.

SAMUEL. You missed a singsong.

JOSS. I bet. Thomas.

> JOSS *enters and sits near his brother, squeezes his arm – they're close*.

THOMAS. Get the wood done?

JOSS. Yeah.

THOMAS. I'll help you shift it tomorrow.

JOSS. What d'you do to your hand, Anne?

ANNE. Just a piece of glass, thanks, Joss.

THOMAS. What we eating?

MA SINGER. What you're given.

JOSS. I can smell chicken.

MA SINGER. For tomorrow. Stew tonight.

SAMUEL. Same as last night.

MA SINGER. Same indeed.

SAMUEL. That window's still not fixed. Can feel the cold coming through on my neck.

JOSS. Should maybe think about fixing it, Sam.

MAY *enters with a large pail of water*.

MA SINGER. May's still to wash.

JOSS. Wash? That water's got ice in it.

MAY. Pass the tub.

JOSS. Ma?

MA SINGER. In here – by the range.

MAY. Room full of people in here.

MA SINGER. It's warmest.

MAY. I /

MA SINGER. / It's only family, we seen it all before.

MAY *pours the water into the tub*.

SAMUEL *stares straight at her, everyone else looks away*.

SAMUEL *pours himself another drink*.

JOSS *grabs* SAMUEL*'s face and jerks it to look the other way*.

JOSS. Keep your eyes on what's yours, Samuel.

SAMUEL *jerks as if to start a fight.* JOSS *puts his hand on his shoulder and keeps him in his seat*.

MAY *takes a rag – bends over the tub – and splashes her face with the water – it's freezing cold – she gasps – she can barely breathe*.

That's enough, that's her done.

MAY, *stubborn and determined, steps into the bath*.

MAY. It's fine.

JOSS. Get out, now.

MAY. I said /

JOSS. / You got a kid in you – get out!

JOSS grabs MAY and lifts her out of the tub and puts a shawl around her.

Long pause in the room.

MA SINGER. Why would you keep a thing like that to yourself?

FANNY. That's a blessing.

ANNE can't speak – starts to sniffle – head down.

JOSS. If it makes it through you'd worry we've not enough to feed it, if it don't – well; it saves everyone the disappointment – doesn't it?

ANNE starts to cry.

SAMUEL. Good, Joss, well done.

–

MAY. So it'll come out dead or hungry?

JOSS. Not if he holds on till spring like he's meant to.

MAY. It'll be winter again before he can walk.

JOSS. You're saying it like I can do something about the seasons, May?

SAMUEL. You'll be right to hold on 'less you want to feed it mud.

JOSS slams the table.

MAY steps into the water – teeth gritted, brave – washes the rest of her body.

JOSS. Get out of there!

MAY keeps going.

MA SINGER grabs MAY out of the water – put the towel around her and makes her warm – holds her.

MA SINGER. Don't go being daft. If I'd a known. Come here.

> ANNE *tries to leave the room.*

Sit down. We're having our dinner.

MAY. I'm sorry, Anne – I didn't want to /

> / FANNY *lays out the meagre selection of food.*

MA SINGER. People celebrate a child. It's a gift.

> ANNE *sobs, tries to make herself stop crying.*

> ANNE *serves, gives* MAY *the food from her plate.*

MAY. Stop it, please.

MA SINGER. You still got to eat, Anne.

ANNE. I've got plenty. You should have it.

> MAY *resists the food.*

JOSS. You're skin and bone, take it.

MAY. Thank you.

> JOSS *puts his hand on the back of* MAY*'s hand – she hooks her thumb over it.*

> *They bow their heads for grace.*

MA SINGER. Bless us, O Lord, and these thy gifts which we are about to receive from thy bounty – through Christ our Lord, Amen.

FAMILY. Amen.

> *They eat.*

SAMUEL. It'll be coming down again tonight, you can tell from the sky.

> MAY *hits the table with the butt of her fork.*

> –

They'll not get in with the coal.

The sound of the bowl being scraped as it's emptied.

We'll lose stock if it's thick.

MAY *hits the table with the butt of her fork.*

FANNY. Any more and we'll be stuck in till spring.

SAMUEL. We'll have to have ourselves a party.

MAY *hits the table hard with the butt of her fork.*

Knock at the door.

Silence. The sons look from one to the other.

–

JOSS. Who's there?

–

FANNY. Too late for deliveries.

MAY *starts for the window.*

JOSS. Sit.

WW (*American accent*). Might I come in?

JOSS. I asked for your name.

JOSS *signals to* THOMAS *to hand him his gun.* THOMAS *gets up.* JOSS *slides his boots on.* THOMAS *passes* JOSS *his gun.*

WW. My name won't help you, sir – you don't know me. I come in good faith. There's no need to be alarmed.

JOSS. You're not from round here?

WW. No, sir; if you'd open the door.

JOSS. Not before I have your name. I don't like shooting strangers, see.

ANNE. Joss!

WW. Mr William Whitcomb.

MAY *stands and to open the door*.

JOSS. Sit down, May? Don't you dare – May?

   MAY *opens the door*.

WW. Good evening. I'm looking for the Singer Farm.

JOSS. You're standing on it.

WW. There's no need for the gun, Mr Singer.

JOSS. You got three of them. Which one do you want?

WW. Whichever one is best placed to do business.

MA SINGER. We don't have no need of business.

MAY. Would you like a cup of tea?

WW. Please, that's kind of you.

   FANNY *takes his hat and coat*. MAY *is fetching the kettle
   from the range*. WW *sees it*.

   That a wood-burning range, Mr Singer?

JOSS. Yes.

WW. It's having some trouble – do you mind if I – take a look?

   WW *steps toward the range and* MRS SINGER *stands up
   and in his way*.

MA SINGER. We'll look after our own range, thank you.

MAY. That accent, if you don't mind me asking?

WW. America.

MAY. You really did walk a long way.

WW. I wonder if you might put the gun down. I wish you and
   your family no harm.

JOSS. I'd like to know the purpose of your visit, Mr Whitcomb.
   We're six miles from anywhere and we're well below
   freezing. It's not the night for a stroll.

THOMAS. What's in the bag?

WW *indicates the range again.*

WW. No coal?

SAMUEL. No delivery this week.

WW *spots* SAMUEL'*s bottle of Scotch –* SAMUEL *pulls it bashfully towards him, unwilling to share.*

WW. Must take you boys days to split enough logs to keep you warm through winter?

THOMAS. Not so long.

MAY *passes him a cup of tea.* WW *blows on the mug – it warms his hands.*

WW. That is quite a comfort, thank you. Those trees take you what? Fifteen years to grow? You're sweating to put your axe through fifteen years and they're only burning for a couple of hours.

JOSS. Plenty of trees in the forest.

WW. Stone Age didn't end for want of stones, Mr Singer.

JOSS. I'd like you to tell us why you /

WW. / May I offer you a demonstration? (*To* ANNE.) Blow out these candles – making a mess all over your walls.

The room is almost entirely dark – save for one or two candles. WW *lifts an apparatus out of his bag and places it on the table.*

JOSS. Mr Whitcomb, I'm a pretty good shot – even in the dark.

WW. I'm sure you are.

WW *lights a match.*

As an illuminator the oil is without a figure – it is the light of the age! Those that have not seen it burn may rest assured its light is no moonshine, but something nearer the clear, strong, brilliant light of day to which darkness is no party!

WW *lights a kerosene lamp. The lamp flame roars. The light lights the room in a way we haven't previously seen.* MAY *steps forward into the pool of light, she's mesmerised.*

SAMUEL is caught – he's been squeezing the back of ANNE's neck cruelly hard in the dark – her eyes are watering – she's crying. SAMUEL – seen – lets go. Steps in.

SAMUEL. Will you look at that?

We see parts of the room – dirt – corners – which we've never seen before. MAY takes a step toward the light – she reaches out to it.

MA SINGER. God Almighty.

MAY holds her hand out to the flame.

MAY. It's warm. It's /

MAY's eyes alight with wonder.

WW. / This here miracle is kerosene – it comes right out of the ground – just like the birds and the bees, the trees and the rivers – it's natural.

JOSS. We got light.

WW. It creates much more heat than whale lamps or wood, it's hotter than coal – and you saw how easy it was to light.

THOMAS. It's expensive, I guess?

WW. Cheaper by half than whale, last three times as long.

A bit of the kerosene has spilt on MAY's finger – she lifts it to her nose and inhales deeply – she loves the smell.

MA SINGER. It smells disgusting.

WW comes in close to MAY – holds her finger up.

WW. That was made when the earth started.

MAY. Imagine being there then?

She turns to him, smiles, transfixed.

WW. There are millions of years, right there on the end of your finger.

MAY. How can a million years fit on one person's finger? Magic?

WW. Near enough.

She breathes it in again.

JOSS. Stop breathing it. It's no good for you.

MAY. I like the smell.

JOSS. Thomas, light the candles.

JOSS *puts his gun down.*

We ain't interested.

WW. I'm not looking to take your money, Mr Singer. I want to buy your land.

JOSS *laughs.*

JOSS. You want to what?

WW. I intend to import into this country and I need land for storage and distribution.

WW *can't take his eyes off* MAY.

JOSS. This farm ain't for sale.

WW. Five hundred pounds.

SAMUEL. Fuck me.

JOSS. This farm is not for sale.

SAMUEL. Five hundred pounds, Joss.

WW. Your brother is a sensible man.

JOSS. That shows how much you know.

WW. Seven hundred pounds.

–

JOSS. This is my land – my family's land. My father and his father before him; it's not for sale.

WW. Eight hundred pounds.

SAMUEL. For God's sake, Joss.

MAY. Joss?

JOSS. I know what needs working and what needs holding off. I can smell a season by the second and I can taste it in the air when death is coming. You hear? I work this land; my children will work this land – and their children after them.

WW. And what will they get from it?

JOSS. If it's what the land can give then it's what we can live off.

MAY. And what if a family grows?

JOSS. Then there will be more hands to work it.

MA SINGER. We accept what God has given and we are grateful for it.

WW. But has God not also given us kerosene? We take trees from the forest without cost. We take air from the sky – water from the river and there is always more water. In America this oil is coming out of the ground faster than we can put it into barrels – we are bleeding it – sweating it in the middle of winter.

MA SINGER. And making a fine profit.

WW. 'Be careful then how you live, not as unwise but as wise, making the most of every opportunity, because these days are evil; therefore do not be foolish, but understand what the Lord's will is' – Ephesians 5:15.

THOMAS. 'From everyone who has been given much, much will be required, and from the one who has been entrusted with much, even more will be asked' – Luke 12:48.

MAY. Eight hundred pounds, Joss.

MA SINGER. Your father turns in his grave to hear his own family sell his home off for some price.

MAY. We could buy new land, a bigger farm, nearby, more cattle – Joss? Not just money but warmth, light – heat – space.

WW. Your family would never be cold or hungry again. This will give you comfort like you cannot imagine.

JOSS. Comfort? Sit like pigs? I didn't spend my whole life working so as I could drink tea and wear hats.

WW. God cannot give comfort?

JOSS *stands and raises his gun at* WW.

JOSS. You'll have my farm over my dead body.

MAY. Joss?

SAMUEL. You won't move him, May.

JOSS. You'd sell in a flash, wouldn't you?

SAMUEL. Yes.

JOSS. You spineless little prick. Show Mr Whitcomb out, May.

WW. I'll be staying at a guesthouse in town until tomorrow evening and the offer will remain on the table in case you change your mind.

JOSS. We won't have time for a trip in town tomorrow; we'll be up feeding cattle.

WW. That is, unless, of course, someone else accepts first. Perhaps your neighbour? And then, Mr Singer – how will you feel about your wife living next door to a man who /

/ WW *puts his hand on* MAY*'s chin and lifts her face up.*

There's something about you.

JOSS *kicks a chair at* WW *and pulls back the safety catch on the gun.*

MAY *steps in front of the door to protect* WW*'s exit.*

JOSS. Move, May!

MAY *steps in front of the gun – so it's close in to her face allowing* WW *to leave behind her.*

Move!

WW *exits.* MAY *stands.* JOSS *lowers his gun.*

THOMAS *takes the gun off* JOSS*, sits him down.*

Pause. Silence.

MAY *goes over to the window – she stares out – can't take her eyes off the black.*

SAMUEL. Close that door, it's bloody freezing in here.

MA SINGER. Beds all round. We're up at dawn.

SAMUEL. Just for a change.

MA SINGER *sets to clearing the table.*

Beds are the only place to get warm.

JOSS. How about you keep your whining trap shut, Sam?

SAMUEL *turns on* JOSS. JOSS *shoves his whisky bottle at him.* SAMUEL *doesn't pick it up.*

MA SINGER. Beds.

JOSS. See, Sam, we need to stay poor so as we need each other. If it came down to just wanting to spend time with folk, you'd be spending a lot of time on your own.

–

They square up.

MA SINGER. But as it is, we're family. (*Beat.*) You're in the woodshed tomorrow, Sam.

JOSS. Why?

MA SINGER. He's hurt his finger.

THOMAS. I'll do the top field with you, Joss, no problem.

SAM *exits with* ANNE.

FANNY *follows them out – kissing* JOSS *on the top of the head as she goes.*

Pa would have done the same.

THOMAS *nods his respect to* JOSS. THOMAS *exits.* MA SINGER *follows out.* JOSS *glares at* MAY.

JOSS. What are you looking at?

MAY *shrugs.*

Pitch black.

MAY. Still.

—

JOSS. You ever argue against me in company again and I'll take my belt to you.

MAY. You never did before.

JOSS. I never had cause before.

—

Come the fuck away from that window. I said.

MAY *goes to him, takes his face in her hands and she kisses him – hard.*

MAY. My blood would run cold without you. I'd die.

JOSS *kisses* MAY, *pulls her into him, sits her on his lap. Rests his head on her chest.*

MAY *lifts his face up to her.*

I know your face better than I know my own.

JOSS. Your hands smell of that stuff.

MAY. Sometimes I think I know it so well I'll see it instead of my own when I look in the mirror.

JOSS. Beard 'n' all?

MAY (*laughs*). Beard 'n' all.

MAY *kisses him.*

–

JOSS. Our lad, he'll get everything we got.

MAY. Might be a girl.

JOSS. Urgh, how horrid.

MAY *pushes* JOSS*'s nose.*

He'll own what he works. He'll never owe anything to no one – just him, the ground and God.

MAY. You're the worst man in the world, you know that, Joss
    Singer?

JOSS. Yeah?

   MAY *shakes her head softly – looks at him like he's gold.*

   Come to bed I'll get you mated.

   MAY *smiles.*

   Is that all right with the – (*Indicates the baby – somehow
   suddenly like a kid himself.*)

MAY (*smiles*). Course.

   MAY *stands and goes back to the window.*

   I might walk a while, else I won't sleep.

JOSS. Walk? You'll freeze.

MAY. Just a minute or two – see the size of the sky.

JOSS. I'll come with you.

MAY. Don't be daft, you go up – I won't be two minutes.

   JOSS *goes to exit, he stops – pours himself a shot of*
   SAMUEL*'s whisky – knocks it back –* MAY *watches.*

   Joss?

JOSS. Hm.

   JOSS *looks up –* MAY *shakes her head, smiles – 'nothing'.*

   JOSS *exits.*

   MAY *goes to the table – the lamp still on it. She dips her*
   finger in the kerosene still on the table, she sniffs it – deep –
   she loves the smell. MA SINGER *stands in the shadows –*
   MAY *doesn't see her.* MAY *goes to the candle and lights her*
   finger. She watches it burn – her eyes wild.

MA SINGER. Careful.

   MAY *jumps – puts it out – looks up.*

   You should take care – in your condition.

MAY. It ever bother you, living down in the valley like this? Hills up on every side? Three days' walk just to see something you ain't used to seein'.

MA SINGER. No.

MAY stares at MA SINGER – something is understood between them.

MAY. Mother does best for her babby.

MA SINGER. Mother does best for the whole house.

Pause.

If you're stepping out – make sure that door is closed behind you.

MA SINGER goes to bed. MAY fetches her shawl and overcoat from the hook – she wraps up a crust of bread and takes SAMUEL's bottle and ties them in a bundle. MAY picks up the address that WW has left on the table. JOSS's hat is on the table. MAY holds it up and sniffs it – deep. MAY lights the lamp – picks it up – opens the door and walks out into the night.

Interscene

A woman steps out into the night
Carrying a single lamp
She walks barefoot across freezing fields
She walks and walks and walks and walks.

She walks through lands, through empires, through time.

A woman walks across a desert.
The air is hot; the night is black.

One newborn baby gasps for breath.
A million newborn babies gasp for breath.

PART TWO

Colonial Residence, Tehran – 1908

*Colonial residence in the Persian desert. It's beautiful – deep
reds, dark wood, golden lamps, rugs, palms, mosaics – a
courtyard with a salon behind. In the salon, a party that is right
at its height. In the courtyard – a buffet table – covered in the
remains of dinner. Crates of booze and food lay about. Lanterns
have been lit, cigarettes smoked, the gramophone is set up –
there's dancing, drinking, smoking, laughing – all is sumptuous
and exciting – we are having the time of our lives.*

*THOMAS is clearing away the remains of dinner, ready to set
up for dessert.*

*We can just about see, on the horizon, the oil wells of Iran.
Working endlessly. The workers, exhausted and hollow-eyed –
finish the day shift and hand over to the night shift. The handover
is seamless – the drilling doesn't cease for a single second.*

MAY appears in the courtyard with AMY at her side.

THOMAS. You can't be here.

MAY. I need your help.

AMY. Mr Thomas?

   AMY *reaches for some food left on the side.*

THOMAS. No, Amy love, that's not yours, don't touch.

MAY. Please, Thomas – I'll work.

AMY. I'm hungry.

THOMAS. There's a party – half the Admiralty have shown up.

MAY. I've been let go from the club without my final month's
   wages. They were meant to cover my passage home.

AMY. Mr Thomas.

MAY. Don't touch.

THOMAS. Why did they sack you?

MAY. I don't know. Can you help?

AMY. Mummy said bad things to Mrs Wilson.

MAY. No I /

THOMAS. / What did you say?

AMY. She kicked her chair.

THOMAS. You did what?

MAY. It's women's bridge at the club and I'm walking with a
    full tray of pink gin and Mrs Wilson, you know – fat one, all
    airs and graces – leans over the table to get, no doubt,
    another bun – and as I'm walking I kick her chair out, by
    mistake mind – so when she sits down there's nothing
    underneath her and she goes over, gin in her face, legs in the
    air – stockings on, no knickers though –

THOMAS. Christ.

MAY. And from being all – (*Posh.*) 'Oh you thur, you girl' –
    she's all like –

    MAY *puts her hands over* AMY*'s ears,* AMY *wriggles.*

    (*Cockney.*) 'You little shitbag!' Shock of it I guess. Demands
    to have me sacked.

THOMAS. But you only kicked over a chair.

MAY. Never wanted to see me again. I can understand that,
    when you're red-faced. You want to get rid but still. I've got
    no money, no ticket home and I'm in the middle of the desert
    with a eight-year-old.

AMY. Mr Thomas, we left too quickly, I couldn't get George.

THOMAS. Any other night, May, but a load of Naval folk are
    in and D'Arcy is jumpy as hell.

MAY. How many times have I opened the bar or made you
    a meal gone midnight?

THOMAS. It's not the same.

MAY. I've been a good friend, Thomas. Haven't I? Please, Thomas.

AMY. I left George behind.

THOMAS. Work tonight, I'll talk to Mr D'Arcy and see if he'll pay you for it.

MAY. And after that?

THOMAS. God's sake, May. Ana is our housekeeper. She does a good job.

MAY. But she's native. You wait till Mr D'Arcy tastes my custard.

THOMAS. Just tonight, and that's it. You'll have to really pull your weight.

MAY. I work. I'm a worker, you know that.

THOMAS. Clear this, re-lay for desserts. They'll be through any second now. Tablecloth, full linens, crockery and cutlery for thirty-five; cakes, flans, pies on one end, trifles and sweets in the middle, cheese and biscuits at the far end – coffee across the back. I'll get Ana to bring you a uniform. What are you going to do with Amy?

AMY. Did I do something wrong?

THOMAS. No, love – not at all. It's just it's grown-up time and your ma's going to need work this evening. You need to be out of the way.

AMY. I'm good at hiding. Aren't I, Thomas?

THOMAS *is looking about for a place.*

MAY. I'll put her under the table.

THOMAS. Are you out of your mind?

MAY. No one is going to look right under their nose and it means she's nearby and I can keep an eye on her.

AMY. George is back at the club. I don't like him sitting there all on his own. He'll be scared.

THOMAS. Mr D'Arcy sees her and my neck's on the line – you hear?

THOMAS *bends down to* AMY.

Where did you leave him?

AMY. Who?

THOMAS. George and his impossibly brilliant red coat?

AMY. I left him on the floor next to our sleeping mats.

THOMAS (*to* MAY). Two bottles of Imperial Brut on the end there.

THOMAS *ruffles her hair and exits.* MAY *throws a tablecloth over the buffet table at double speed, smooths the top and makes sure it's equal on all sides.*

MAY. Do you remember how good girls, if they sit very quietly, get extra dates at breakfast?

AMY. Yes.

MAY *puts* AMY *under the table.*

She takes a chair and sits at the table – she takes a breath then sets to work, folding each of the napkins into a perfect oblong and then tying each with a piece of velvet, tied into a bow. The work is repetitive, precise – exacting – there is a rhythm to it, it may be dainty but it is gruelling in its way.

ANA *enters.* ANA *holds out a waitress outfit to* MAY.

MAY. Thank you.

ANA. باید این را بپوشی. (*Bāyad īn rā bepūshī.*) [You need to put it on.]

MAY. I don't understand.

ANA. من نمیفهمم. (*Man nemīfahmam.*) [I don't understand.]

MAY. I'm sorry – I don't understand.

ANA. باید این را بپوشی. (*Bāyad īn rā bepūshī*.) [You need to put it on.]

MAY. I'm sorry – I don't understand you.

ANA. من تو را نمیفهمم. (*Man tū rā nemīfahmam*.) [I don't understand you.]

The women stare at each other a moment.

AMY *sticks her head out from under the cloth.*

ANA *sees her and pulls her out a bit – she looks at her face – kisses her head.*

MAY. Do you mind, I /

AMY. / من فکر نمیکردم که تو اینجا باشی. (*Man fekr nemikardam keh tū īnjā bāshī*.) [I didn't know you would be here.]

ANA. خوشحالم که میبینمت امی جان. (*Khūshḥālam keh mībīnamet Amy Jān*.) [It's nice to see you, Amy.]

MAY *pulls* AMY *away from* ANA.

MAY (*to* AMY). I've told you about speaking Farsi.

ANA. با بچه های من بازی میکند. ما نزدیک باشگاه زندگی میکنیم, در شهر. (*Bā bacheh hāye man bāzī mīkonad. Mā nazdīke bāshgāh zendegī mīkonīm, dar shahr*.) [She plays with my children – we live near to the club, in town.]

MAY. I don't understand you.

AMY. Ana's garden is next to the club's garden and she has Yusuf, he's my friend.

MAY. I should get on.

ANA. خوشحالم که ما میتوانیم کمک کنیم. (*Khūshḥālam keh mā mītavānīm komak konīm*.) [I'm glad we can help.]

MAY *puts* AMY *back under the table and turns back to the napkins*. ANA *goes back into the party – she does secret waves to* AMY *over her shoulder that* MAY *sees.*

AMY. I want George.

MAY. Shh.

> AMY *whines*.

> We'll get you a new George, how about that?

AMY. That's a horrid thing to say.

MAY. George was very dirty and old.

AMY. He's there on his own.

MAY. We can't go back. (*Beat*.) You are too old for stuffed toys.
They're for little girls, silly little girls. You're not a little girl
any more – do you hear?

AMY. I want Ana, she's a nicer mother than you are.

MAY. Stay under there and no noise – do you hear? I'm trying
to – I'm – trying.

> MAY *puts* AMY *under the table*. MAY *goes to look at the
> champagne bottles. She doesn't know which is which.*

> Amy?

AMY. I'm hiding.

MAY. Come here.

AMY. Thomas said to /

MAY. / Just for a minute.

> AMY *comes out and stands by her mum*.

> (*Looking at champagne*.) Imperial Brut.

AMY. 'I' like a big straight tree, 'B' like half a butterfly.

> AMY *picks it out and hands it to* MAY. MAY *opens her
> dress and gives* AMY *a few pieces of food she's stolen,
> looking over her shoulder the whole time.*

> (*Still under the table*.) Mrs Murray at the club did reading
> with me /

MAY. / Shh.

AMY. She said I'm clever with a capital C.

MAY *stops a second – overwhelmed with pride.*

MAY. She said what?

AMY. She said I can get a scholarship to a posh school in London if we can pay for a tutor.

MAY *takes* AMY *out – holds her close – stares into her eyes.*

MAY. We'll find a way. I promise. What's our house going to look like?

AMY. White square, four windows and a rose bush and a garden path that goes all the way down to the sea. Splosh.

MAY. And you're going to go to a good school and we'll stay in evenings, cosy by the fire and eat big dinners, just us two?

AMY. Why don't we have a family?

MAY. We do, you and me – we're a family.

AMY. When I told Ana we only had two family she laughed –

MAY. I'm not sure you'd like sleeping in a room of twenty people.

AMY. Yes, I would.

MAY. Take a deep breath in.

AMY *takes a breath in.*

AMY *nods.*

(*Whilst holding her breath and still working impossibly quickly.*) Quietly.

They both let out sounds, any sound – but long with all the breath. AMY *rolls around laughing.*

AMY. You sounded like a fart. Why are you crying?

MAY. I'm not crying.

AMY. You look like you're crying.

MAY. You know when you're older I think you're going to be glad that we did brave things. We'll find a new place, better than the club and it will pay more and /

AMY. / It's not brave if you're crying.

MAY. I know.

AMY. You're not allowed to cry, you're a grown-up.

> SAMUEL *enters.* AMY *dashes back under the table just in time.* SAMUEL *doesn't see her.*

MAY. Can I help you, sir?

SAMUEL. Champagne?

MAY. I'll bring some out to you.

SAMUEL. I'll get it if you just let me know…

> MAY *points to the champagne.*

Bit warm. Officer Samuel – British Admiralty. Interloper, party-goer, aggravator, aviator.

> *He offers her his hand.* MAY*'s hands are full of the napkins.*

MAY. What does all that mean?

SAMUEL. No idea really. Nonsense, mostly.

MAY. Sounds exciting.

SAMUEL. Does it?

MAY. Very.

> SAMUEL *smiles at* MAY, MAY *smiles at* SAMUEL.

SAMUEL. Haven't you got a lovely smile?

> MAY *fluffs a napkin and curses.*

MAY. Shit.

> THOMAS *enters and coughs over the swear word.*

THOMAS. Can I help you, Officer Samuel?

SAMUEL. I was after a bottle of cold champagne.

THOMAS. I'll bring one out.

SAMUEL. It's daft but I wanted to look as if I got it. To be carrying it – like I knew where to find it. Just makes me look more.

THOMAS. Right. Well – I'll fetch you a bottle.

THOMAS *exits*.

SAMUEL *watches* MAY *a little while*.

SAMUEL. Nimble fingers.

MAY. Practice makes perfect.

–

SAMUEL *watches some more* – MAY *stumbles*.

SAMUEL. Oops.

MAY. Oops.

They laugh.

SAMUEL. Aren't they for wiping our faces?

MAY. No one ever really uses them.

SAMUEL. Then why are you tying them with such a tiny pretty bow?

THOMAS *re-enters with the bottle* – *hands it to* SAMUEL.

Much appreciated. You're a champion.

SAMUEL *exits*.

THOMAS. And you're an absolute arsehole of a man.

SAMUEL *re-enters*.

SAMUEL. It's Mr Thomas, isn't it?

THOMAS. Yes, Officer Samuel.

SAMUEL. You couldn't open it for me? I can't get the wire thing off.

SAMUEL *hands* THOMAS *the bottle*. THOMAS *gets the wire thing off*.

It's charming out here, isn't it?

THOMAS. By the buffet?

SAMUEL. Persia – the desert, so much… sand – it'd kill you in how many days walking, do you think?

THOMAS. Don't know – you'd have to try it.

SAMUEL. The hot night air… It's – all so promising. Don't you think? You should see the faces of the natives when we showed them some new gear this afternoon, like they were watching magic. And to top it all, you're on the other side of the world and there's still bloody good champagne. What more could you want?

MAY *smiles at him.*

MAY. You're having a nice time, aren't you?

SAMUEL. Truth be told – it's all stiff colonels and podgy wives – oh wait, I mean – stiff wives and podgy – hm.

MAY *giggles.*

Thanks for this, old chap. I've got some arms to bend and it always helps to have a little leverage.

THOMAS. My pleasure.

SAMUEL *exits.* MAY *keeps working.* THOMAS *glares at the way he went.*

He thinks he's something doesn't he? The shine on his face – like he takes a chamois to it.

MAY. Really?

THOMAS. He walks like the world's going to end without him. Even to the pisser.

MAY. He seemed – gentle, somehow.

THOMAS. He was being a gal-sneeker with you.

MAY. He wasn't? Was he?

THOMAS. Naval officers are. The things I've seen those men do after hours, it's not – very nice. And now they're walking around like they're running the place. There's going to be trouble. May, your hands – the napkins. Tch.

MAY. What?

THOMAS. There's blood.

MAY. Shit. It's the bleach at the club – sorry.

THOMAS. We can't put them out with blood on them.

MAY. It's fine – look, we'll turn them over – no one will notice, too drunk to feel their faces let alone wipe them.

Piles and piles and plates and plates of deserts get bought through – they're obscene – huge – wild – colourful – MAY *can't believe her eyes. She has to shove* AMY *under the table quite forcefully to get her out of the way in time.* THOMAS *helps bring the cake in and lingers a little when they've all been placed – checking the table but really enjoying the time with* MAY, *you get half the sense that he might be building up to something.*

Could feed you for weeks.

THOMAS *sort of half-flirty raises his eyebrows at her. She's unreceptive to it – very different from the effect of* SAMUEL.

What?

THOMAS *wants subtext; he's trying to do what he saw* SAMUEL *do but* MAY *won't accommodate it. He tries to infer again – eyebrows, cheeky smile.*

What does that mean?

THOMAS. You know you want to.

THOMAS *does it again.*

MAY. I don't know what you're asking.

THOMAS *does it again.*

What?

THOMAS. You can sneak a bit, if you want. Just a little bit though.

MAY *is intimidated but takes some cake – as if it's precious – she goes to put it in her mouth, ready to relish it.*

> THOMAS *swipes a bit of the icing. He laughs.* MAY *doesn't laugh.* MAY *puts the cake down, goes back to work.*

MAY. You have it.

THOMAS. I only took a bit.

MAY. I wasn't really hungry anyway.

THOMAS. I was just joking.

MAY. I know, it's not a problem – you go ahead, it's yours now.

THOMAS. Just because I touched it?

MAY. Don't be silly, of course not.

THOMAS. Have it.

MAY. No.

THOMAS. Why?

MAY. It's spoilt.

THOMAS. Why?

> MAY *goes back to work.* THOMAS *angry in some way – pushes the cake into the bin.*

> I'm not happy about Amy being in here whilst there are guests around.

MAY. She's been fine.

THOMAS. I'll take her out and leave her with Ana.

MAY. I want her with me.

THOMAS. You're working.

AMY. Where are we going?

MAY. Thomas!

THOMAS. We're going to find Ana.

AMY. Yes.

THOMAS. I need you to stay where you are, that needs to be manned.

MAY. Amy? Amy, love?

> THOMAS *and* AMY *exit.* MAY *stands behind the buffet. She can't bear it – she can't stand this life. She needs her daughter. She almost breaks.* MAY *takes a single slice of her own cake, arranges it perfectly, goes to take a single, perfect mouthful –* SAMUEL *enters – and catches her.*

SAMUEL. Naughty.

> MAY *jumps out of her skin.*

Don't mind me, as you were. I'm just having a breather. Have you got a light?

> MAY *goes to put the cake down.*

I'll get them, just point.

> MAY *points to the matches – and continues with her mouthful. She's somehow able to enjoy the mouthful with him in the room – it feels oddly independent and mutual, it's nice.* SAMUEL *looks at her*

> *The sound of a motorcar starting out in the front.* MAY *jumps – terrified, gasps –* SAMUEL *laughs.*

MAY. Sorry, can't get used to them. Scare the living daylights out of me.

SAMUEL. You don't look scared.

MAY. What do you mean?

SAMUEL. You don't look scared. Your eyes – they're all lit up.

MAY. Are they?

> MAY *smiles –* SAMUEL *smiles.*

SAMUEL. There is something about the sound of a motorcar in the middle of the desert. Isn't there? It absolutely shouldn't be there and yet – in all that silence, it's so commanding.

The sound of the car rises, SAMUEL *hovers his hand on the centre of her chest, it's not predatory yet – it's commanding – almost perfunctory.*

Can you feel it? Through the soles of your feet?

MAY. Yes.

MAY *smiles up at him.*

SAMUEL. Women love an engine.

MAY. Do they?

SAMUEL. 'Do they?' – come on, don't give me that – look at you.

MAY *shrugs – holds his eye, challenging.*

What is it? I'm interested – what is it about a motorcar that is so attractive?

MAY. I don't know.

SAMUEL. It can turn one teaspoon of oil into the strength of two hundred men.

MAY. That seems incredible.

SAMUEL. Is that it? The power of two hundred men?

MAY. The power is in the teaspoon of oil not the man though, isn't it? An invalid could drive a motorcar.

SAMUEL. Ha! Ha! I love it – I should go and tell the Colonel, that'd make him spit. Do you know, today, we – the Admiralty have put men in the sky? You'd never have dreamt of it.

MAY. What's going on in there? What gets said?

SAMUEL. What's your name?

MAY. May.

SAMUEL. Do you ever think you were born at exactly the right moment? That we are going to see the very best of it. You and I, May – right here, right now – in the hot wind of this night, are standing in a moment of time where the speed and degree of mankind's progress is unprecedented. No one has felt like this before.

MAY *smiles, he's got her*.

MAY. The way you talk – the things you're talking about – it's as if you speak and whole bits of the world are moving. I talk about tea towels or glasses.

SAMUEL. Tea towels.

MAY. It doesn't suit you.

SAMUEL (*faux cockney*). Tea towel.

MAY. Tell me, please.

SAMUEL. The Kaiser has built oil-powered ships, so we build oil-powered ships. But we don't have any oil.

MAY. Why not?

SAMUEL. Damned bad luck. There's no oil anywhere in the Empire. Maybe, God had a good laugh when he dealt the stuff out, gave it to all the hardest-to-reach places invariably run by a bunch of backward savages; putting his favourite pupils through their paces, know what I mean? So – we need to buy it from somewhere. It's my job to get hold of Persian oil. Hence the bubbly and the faint whiff of panic.

–

MAY. You're the British Government – you can do what you like. Can't you?

SAMUEL. Usually you see these stupid girls, just standing there with their hands folded in front of them looking barely fucking sentient. (*Beat*.) If the British Government owns the drilling company and tribesmen break the pipelines, say, the British Government has to punish those tribesmen.

MAY. Yes?

SAMUEL. That would be an act of dominion. It would be an invasion. But what's a fellow meant to do? If we don't have full control anyone can fuck us when our back's against the wall. Can't they? You'd think they'd be grateful – we're bringing money and education and /

/ MAY hands SAMUEL the drink.

MAY. Your hand is shaking.

SAMUEL. No it's not.

MAY puts her hand on it.

MAY. Shh.

SAMUEL pulls away.

SAMUEL. I do wish staff wouldn't overstep.

THOMAS enters, unseen.

Mr Thomas – I um, was just having some cake – May here is quite /

THOMAS. / Isn't she.

SAMUEL. I should get back in there.

MAY. You should.

THOMAS. Persia is not British land.

SAMUEL. The one quality that I cannot abide in my staff is indiscretion.

THOMAS. I'm sure. The Shah is fifteen years old – your lot have been filling him full of sweets and champagne for months, I can see what you're doing. You buy off D'Arcy and you drug a child with sweets and concubines /

SAMUEL. / Mr Thomas, you do not speak to an officer in that tone /

THOMAS. / Have you seen the size of him?

SAMUEL. You have all the self-righteousness afforded to a man with very little influence. You have no sense of the compromise that responsibility demands. It makes you seem very – young.

THOMAS. When Mr D'Arcy first struck, he came back to the
house that night. He sat out on that veranda – stared out
across the land. I took him a drink; his face was wet with
tears, he says – 'I have just unleashed unthinkable
misfortune on Persia, haven't I?' I told him not to be daft.
He knew. He knew.

MAY. I need to get this table tidied up if you two gentlemen
could /

THOMAS. / You'll pay them nothing and work them like dogs.

SAMUEL. You're not sounding frightfully patriotic.

THOMAS. The Persian people are proud – they will rise up.

SAMUEL. If we can win a war, I dare say a few tribesmen
shouldn't be a problem. If you'll excuse me, I have work
to do.

SAMUEL *knocks back his Scotch, raises his glass to*
THOMAS.

God save the King.

SAMUEL *exits back through into the party.*

THOMAS. What are you doing?

MAY. Can you hold the fort for two minutes whilst I go and get
Amy. I don't like her with that girl.

THOMAS. Her name is Ana.

MAY. I want Amy where I can see her.

MAY *tries to leave* – THOMAS *steps in her way – stops her
– catches her by the arm.*

THOMAS. Listen – to me, okay? There's something I want
to say – I've been wanting to say. I need to get it all out or
I won't get it out at all. I think we get on – I was glad you
came here this evening – that you came to me – I.

MAY. Thomas.

THOMAS. It wouldn't be nothing for me to marry a single
woman with a child, it would be a small injury – but I

wouldn't mind, see? I've got the space – a spare room for the little one and – I've a little saved if you wanted a wedding or anything for the child. We could go home together. It's a cottage, it's a small village – there's a local school. We could be happy. It's not a lot but it's – I'd never let you down. I wouldn't touch you unless you asked. I. I care for you and for Amy.

THOMAS *goes in to kiss her – she sort of half takes it but doesn't really want it. She stiffens – it's unwanted but very bravely offered.*

Your hands are bleeding; you've got no wage; you've got no way home.

MAY. I know, I just. I.

THOMAS. Why can't you – just – relent? No one doubts your strength, May.

MAY. I left a man I loved so much, I thought I was going to die. I didn't die. It's got to have been worth something. It makes no sense to compromise now.

THOMAS. How do you expect to live your life without compromise?

MAY. If it isn't love then I might as well make the best life I can for my child.

THOMAS. It depends what you mean by best, I suppose.

MAY. She can get schooling. Walk into any room and feel like she's meant to be there – know which fork to use, what words to say.

THOMAS. You're going to be peddling under the table at a million miles an hour for the rest of your life. You don't belong.

MAY. You don't get to tell me where I belong!

THOMAS. I can give you a home.

MAY. You'd have a woman come and live with you knowing that she doesn't love you?

SAMUEL *enters – he watches from the shadows.*

–

THOMAS *goes again – steps towards her and tries to kiss her –* MAY *tries this time – really tries – holds her head still and takes the kiss – but no, breaks away – can't do it.*

I'm sorry – I'm a bit cold.

THOMAS *steps toward* MAY *again.* SAMUEL *interrupts.*

SAMUEL. Mr Thomas, the woman has made it clear that she doesn't want to be touched.

THOMAS *turns to leave.*

No, wait.

THOMAS. I have duties to attend to.

SAMUEL. You owe May an apology.

THOMAS. I really do have to /

/ SAMUEL *steps in close – puts his hand on* THOMAS*'s shoulder.*

MAY. It's fine, I /

SAMUEL. / I'd like you to apologise.

–

SAMUEL *rests with his hand on* THOMAS*'s shoulder.*

Come on, Mr Thomas.

THOMAS. I'm sorry, May.

MAY. I need to finish the /

SAMUEL. / For touching a lady when she didn't ask?

THOMAS. I'm sorry for touching you when you didn't ask.

MAY. It's fine, I – it's really no /

SAMUEL. / Good, Thomas, good.

SAMUEL *grasps his shoulder reassuringly – slaps him solidly on the arm – they hold one another's eye a moment.* MAY *can't bear it – looks away.*

AMY *enters.*

AMY. I had a bad dream. I had a dream, Mr Thomas – there was a man, he was walking in the desert and he was burning.

—

THOMAS. It's okay. Hey, I've got something for you.

THOMAS *produces George the teddy bear – he's old and battered and in a red coat, but he's really lovely.* AMY *grabs him with glee.*

AMY. Why were you being told off?

THOMAS (*to* AMY, *but really to* MAY *and* SAMUEL). When you're making your mind up – if it feels like eels in there and it makes that – (*Points to her head.*) go like the clappers – don't do it. You want – slow and knowing, like God feels – in there – (*Points to her stomach.*) and clean and sharp, like the first wind of autumn in there. (*Points to her head.*)

MAY. What if clappers and eels is fear and on the other side is better than you ever imagined.

AMY. Don't go. Mr Thomas – please don't go.

THOMAS (*holds up two envelopes*). This is your pay for this evening, and Ana's pay for the month. Make sure she gets it? He's paid you both in pounds, it's worth more.

THOMAS *exits.*

SAMUEL. Whose is this little one, eh?

AMY *glares at him.*

I've got your nose.

AMY. No you haven't.

SAMUEL. Yes, I have. Look – it's my nose now!

AMY. That's just your thumb.

SAMUEL (*to* MAY). Tough crowd. (*To* AMY.) It's well past your bedtime, why don't you go and ask kind Mr Thomas to find your parents. Hm?

AMY. Mummy.

AMY *moves over to* MAY.

–

MAY. Officer Samuel, this is Amy – my daughter. Amy, say hello to Officer Samuel.

AMY. Hello.

SAMUEL. Hello.

AMY. I don't like you.

MAY. Amy!

SAMUEL. Let's see what we can do about that, shall we?

SAMUEL *takes a huge decorative box off the back of the table – it's wrapped in a beautiful shawl – he opens and reveals Turkish delight – it smells amazing; it looks amazing. He offers her one – she's nervous to take one – she reaches; he slaps her hand playfully.*

I'm only joking – go on.

AMY. It smells like roses.

SAMUEL. If it smells like roses, just imagine what it will taste like.

AMY *takes a piece – she thinks it's delicious – she starts rolling around with joy. She drops George.*

You see?

AMY *looks up into* SAMUEL's *face.*

AMY. You look tired.

SAMUEL. I am rather.

AMY. Can I have another one?

MAY. No, that's enough.

SAMUEL. One more won't hurt.

AMY *reaches for the Turkish delight.* SAMUEL *hands the box to her without thinking.* SAMUEL *goes in close to* MAY.

What are a single woman and her child doing out here on their own?

MAY. I wanted to show her the world.

SAMUEL. A little reckless, no?

MAY. They said there was money coming out of the ground.

SAMUEL. And is there?

MAY. For some.

SAMUEL. Who's her father?

MAY. The very best of men.

SAMUEL. The best? Surely not.

MAY. The best.

SAMUEL. Left you in the lurch?

MAY. A wife would add respectability to an officer that had to take charge of a concession in a Muslim country. No?

SAMUEL. Not if she had a bastard child.

MAY. A widow? Why not?

SAMUEL. First he's the best of men and now he's dead.

MAY *shrugs.*

All this wife business – how is a fellow meant to enjoy a game if he's already won?

MAY. I – I didn't /

SAMUEL. / Ease up, eh?

MAY. I, like you, know what I'm worth, Mr Samuel.

SAMUEL. Officer Samuel.

MAY. My mistake, forgive me.

MAY *adjusts* SAMUEL*'s jacket for him.*

SAMUEL. What is it?

MAY. It's a little big across the shoulders, that's all. There we go, that's better. Do you know what, I think I would like a piece of cake.

SAMUEL. You're still on duty, aren't you?

MAY. I don't know, am I?

MAY *reaches for the cake.*

SAMUEL. Use a fork, come along, you've been scrabbling around all day.

MAY *takes the fork from* SAMUEL *– goes for a piece of cake.* SAMUEL *goes in for it –* MAY *pulls away.* SAMUEL *picks something up and dusts* MAY*'s nose with it. It's all a bit of a scrabble – he wants her; she resists it.*

ANA *enters – she doesn't see* AMY. ANA *starts clearing up the table.*

ANA *looks at* MAY *then keeps her eyes on the ground, she's awkward about watching but the work needs to be done.*

You look like a bear, like a little snow bear. Come on – open, open sesame.

MAY. You're being silly.

SAMUEL. If I couldn't be silly with my wife who could I be silly with?

MAY. Officer Samuel? The girl is right there.

SAMUEL *goes to grab* MAY. *She tries to push him off but he really goes for it – runs his hand up her leg.*

AMY (*with her mouth full*). Mummy.

MAY *suddenly spots* AMY *who had stuffed her face entirely with the Turkish delight – it's horrible somehow, she looks like she's going to be sick.*

MAY. Amy!

SAMUEL. Leave her, she's fine – for a moment, just leave her.

MAY. Amy!

MAY *is trying to wriggle free of* SAMUEL *to get to* AMY, *but he's holding tight.* ANA *goes over to* AMY – *gets there first – tries to help.* MAY *arrives and pushes her off.*

She's my child! I'll deal with it – she's my child.

ANA *steps back.*

Amy, spit it out – Amy! Spit it out! Stop – spit them out – you're going to be sick. Spit – spit them into my hand.

AMY (*mouth full*). No.

MAY. Amy! Spit them out.

AMY. I don't want to.

MAY. You're going to be sick. Stop it!

AMY *tries to swallow them.*

MAY *grabs her and puts her hand into her mouth to take the sweets out,* AMY *resists.*

Don't.

SAMUEL *grabs* AMY *hard and smacks her – until she spits them out.* MAY *watches in horror – but doesn't intervene.* AMY *starts wailing, wailing – crying.* SAMUEL, *slightly absent-mindedly, picks up the teddy and gives it back to* AMY. MAY *can barely look at her she feels so guilty.* ANA *tries to go to* AMY.

Leave her.

AMY. Ana! Ana!

SAMUEL. She has to learn her lesson or she'll do it again and cause herself harm.

SAMUEL *takes the cloth from the Turkish delight and wraps it around* AMY's *head –* ANA *flinches forward.* MAY *glares at her.*

Now come on, cheer up. Why don't you do us a little dance?
Hm? Dance like Ana dances? No? We can all be little
dancers.

ANA. نگذار بهش دست بزند. (*Nagzār behesh dast bezanad.*) [Don't let
him touch her.]

AMY *stays really still.*

SAMUEL. Show her how to dance.

ANA. من نمیفهمم. (*Man nemīfahmam.*) [I don't understand.]

SAMUEL *imitates a little dance – asks* ANA *to do it.*

SAMUEL. I said, dance. I've seen you dance. I know you know
how to do it.

SAMUEL *looks long at* ANA, *we can feel the history and it's
not good.*

ANA *doesn't move.*

AMY *looks nervously at her mum and starts dancing.*

ANA. No.

SAMUEL *loves it – he hoots and stares. He goes to touch*
AMY. ANA *dives in and pulls* AMY *away from* SAMUEL.

SAMUEL. It's not your place /

MAY. / Come here, Ames.

ANA. نگذار برود نزدیک دخترت. (*Nagzār beravad nazdīke dokhtaret.*)
[Don't let him near your daughter.]

SAMUEL. Why don't you both come back with me to Tehran
this evening. Bring the child – I've got staff who can keep an
eye on her.

MAY. I –

SAMUEL. Just wait until you see my residence – you'd have
the run of the place. Yes?

MAY. Yes?

MAY *offers her hand for* SAMUEL *to shake it – they shake.*

You get your things and we'll meet you out the front.

SAMUEL *squeezes* ANA *on the back of the neck as he goes – MAY doesn't see. It should echo the gesture in Part One.* SAMUEL *exits.*

AMY. Where are we going now?

MAY. On an adventure.

MAY *reaches for the two envelopes that* THOMAS *left with the wages in them.*

ANA *watches her.*

ANA. No.

MAY. Sorry?

ANA. Mine.

MAY. No – this is for me.

ANA. My money.

MAY. It's in pounds, look. Thomas said he'd give you yours later – in rial. See.

ANA. من نمیفهمم. (*Man nemīfahmam.*) [I don't understand.]

ANA *grabs for the money.*

MAY. No – no, it's mine. It's in pounds – you can't use this. This is useless to you. He will give you yours in rial.

ANA. خواهش میکنم از مادرت بپرس این پول من است. (*Khāhesh mīkonam az mādaret bepors īn pūle man ast.*) [Please – ask your mother, is that my money?]

AMY. Is that her money?

AMY *looks up into her mother's face.*

MAY. No.

AMY *shakes her head at* ANA.

AMY. خداحافظ انا. (*Khodāḥāfeẓ Ana.*) [Bye bye, Ana.]

MAY. You should speak to them in English, if you've got the chance to educate them – you owe it to them to do so.

MAY *takes* AMY *and leads her out the opposite way to where* SAMUEL *went. They wait for* SAMUEL *to re-enter looking for them – and then run.*

SAMUEL. Where are they?

ANA *stares at* SAMUEL. *She's been eating cake.* THOMAS *enters – he sees the intent of* SAMUEL.

Where are they?

ANA. من نمیفهمم. (*Man nemīfahmam.*) [I don't understand.]

THOMAS *looks at* ANA, *turns away – exits.*

SAMUEL *approaches* ANA *with malice.*

MAY. You're going to have to be brave for a little bit longer, okay?

AMY. Why?

MAY. We're going to go in a motorcar.

AMY. With Mr Thomas?

MAY. No.

AMY. With Officer Samuel?

MAY. No.

AMY. Who with?

MAY. Just us – just you and me, like a little team. Okay?

AMY. You're holding too tight. Stop it – you're holding too tight. Let go.

The sound of a motorcar rises – they've nicked the car – they speed off across the desert. AMY *is sick.*

Interscene

The sound of an engine –
The sound of a thousand engines
Come trucks, come trains, come tanks.
Come gunfire.

A small army of Iranian men walk obediently, in line, like ants –
across the scorching sand; off to work the well.

Headlights across a desert.
A woman drives.

She drives and drives and drives and drives
Through days and nights,
Past towns and street lights –
She drives
And drives
Through time
To get the kids home before bed.

PART THREE

Detached House, Hampstead – 1970

*A nice, detached, slightly-larger-than-average house, in
Hampstead. Four windows, a rose bush, a path. The kitchen –
something of Edward Hopper, lit – electric, Formica, sterile.
MAY, forties, enters and drops her briefcase under the kitchen
table; she puts her car keys on the countertop. She opens the
fridge – nibbles something. Pours herself a drink – she opens
the washing machine – takes out the washing takes it through to
the utility room.*

*AMY, fifteen, and NATE, sixteen, enter. They get drinks, snacks
– they don't notice the car keys. They sit on the kitchen table.
MAY enters, but stands in the shadow of the doorway, realises
she hasn't been seen. MAY watches.*

NATE. We'd have a baby and live in a little house in the middle
of a field in the middle of nowhere – we'd wake up in the
morning and see loads of sky.

We'd work hard in the daytime and grow food – we'd sit on
the porch in the night-time and read books, we'd all sleep in
one room, we'd go to sleep listening to each other breathing.
We'd get annoyed, it'd be hard but it'd be good.

We'd know everyone. You'd know people in the street and
they'd bring food for you if I got sick and food for me if you
got sick and I'd help people fix things and you'd help look
after their kids and big meals and harvest and carol singing –
you know?

NATE *starts kissing* AMY.

MAY *enters the room to stop them.*

NATE *puts his hand up* AMY*'s skirt.*

MAY *steps back into her hiding place.*

NATE encourages AMY, *slightly clumsily, to lie back on to the kitchen table.* NATE *gets a chair, sits at one end of the table and goes down on* AMY.

AMY. Not here – what if /

NATE. / It's wild; it's like being outside.

It's really not. NATE*'s head is hidden between* AMY*'s legs.* AMY*'s face turns outward to the audience.* AMY*'s expression speaks to awkwardness and slight discomfort but mostly to being profoundly underwhelmed. We stay like this for some time.* MAY *coughs, turns on the lights.* AMY *and* NATE *scramble for chairs, objects, their lives.* MAY *puts the shopping bags up on the counter and starts unpacking them.*

MAY. Hello.

NATE. Hi, Miss Singer. I'm Nate.

AMY. My boyfriend.

MAY. Are you staying for dinner, Nate – or have you already eaten?

NATE. I'm – I'm – I don't mind, I'm not very hungry – I /

AMY. / He'd love to stay. What are we having?

MAY unpacks supermarket bag.

MAY. Chicken Kiev. Dauphinoise potatoes. We agreed, remember? I'd be home by six and we'd eat together, just us.

AMY. There's no green.

MAY throws peas out of the bag.

MAY puts the chicken into the microwave – sets the timer. Turns on the kettle.

MAY. Peas. Have you two finished with the table?

NATE. Yeah. Sure. Yeah.

AMY. No.

MAY. Well, I need to do some work.

AMY. You said you were going to do work at work and home at
    home from now on. You promised.

NATE. I wish my mum worked.

MAY. Look at that, darling, see – you should be grateful.

AMY. Nate's mum let him put a sticker on their thermostat
    saying 'turn it down one degree can save the world'.

NATE. I put another one on my light switch saying 'save energy
    drink your own piss' and she made me take it down which is
    totally fucked because, a) it's my light switch in my room,
    and b) it's clearly a joke.

AMY. I think I should get a say as to what happens in the house
    I have to live in.

MAY. Tell me about it.

AMY. Or I'll move out.

MAY. With one and six in your back pocket?

AMY. Nate's got savings.

MAY. If he ships you out of this house I will have him done for
    statutory quicker than he can blink.

NATE. What's stat– /

AMY. / Don't.

MAY. Not that you really strike me as a – shipper, particularly,
    Nate.

AMY. I don't think the kitchen table I have to eat off should be
    used for capitalist scheming.

–

MAY *raises her eyebrows at* AMY.

MAY. Would you like a beer – just one – won't hurt, will it?

NATE. Um, thanks.

AMY. Classic case of a capitalist monster offering incentives to
    distract the general public from opposing /

MAY. / You don't feel very general, darling, you feel quite specific. Can you lay the table please?

AMY. See.

NATE. I'll do it if you like.

NATE *picks up the plates and knives and forks and starts laying the table.* MAY *watches him a moment with concern, he stumbles something.*

MAY. Are you an activist, Nate?

NATE. I am – but only for, like, some issues. I feel a lot about whales.

MAY. The country?

NATE. The animal.

AMY. Mum's company causes corruption and /

MAY. / That's not true.

AMY. She provides foreign investment to countries that lack the proper infrastructure to /

NATE. / Is infrastructure like infrared?

MAY. No, Nate – no, it's not.

AMY. Don't say it like that.

MAY. Like what?

AMY. Don't be unkind.

MAY *stops, genuinely challenged, looks at her daughter.*

MAY. I wasn't. If it seemed like I was then I apologise.

NATE. How was she being unkind?

–

AMY. Let alone the fact that you're taking *a fossil – a fossil –* do you ever think about that, Mum? *A fossil –*

MAY. Yes, I heard.

AMY. *A fossil –*

MAY. Oh God. (*Rolls her eyes.*)

AMY. Every drop of oil that you drag out of the ground contains billions of tiny sea creatures and took one hundred and fifty million years to make – and you get to decide how it's used, do you? Out of six million generations – you know best? You put it in your car to get to the shops a bit quicker?

MAY. To buy you dinner.

AMY. I'm not hungry.

MAY. Well, we've got to eat. Put the chicken in the oven, would you, darling?

AMY *gives the oven door an almighty thwack as she closes it.*

NATE. Careful, babe, Desperate Dan.

NATE *catches* AMY*'s eye – they giggle – they're enjoying this.*

MAY. What's Desperate Dan?

AMY. Nothing.

MAY. What is it?

NATE. Oh he's just a /

AMY. / It's nothing – young person's stuff.

MAY. Durex.

NATE *stumbles a plate.*

Careful, Nate.

AMY. What?

MAY. Durex – lubricant – KY Jelly and even Vaseline if you're on a budget and – actually – now I come to think of it, the contraceptive pill.

NATE. It's important to be safe.

MAY. All made of oil.

AMY *storms out of the room.*

There's no point storming off, your supper is almost ready
and you'll only have to slink back in and that's twice as
awkward for everyone. Nate?

NATE. Yes?

MAY. What do you think about /

/ AMY *re-enters. Fire in her eyes, she's carrying a cigarette
packet.*

Oh look here she is – salt and pepper and a jug of water
please.

AMY *sits up at the kitchen counter – on a high stool and
takes a cigarette out of the packet – and lights it.* NATE
watches with horror.

Small beat.

MAY *watches her.*

—

AMY. Maybe we could go to the pictures this evening, darling?
What do you think?

NATE. You talking to me?

AMY. Yes. Darling.

MAY *leans over and takes a cigarette out of* AMY*'s packet.*

MAY *beckons for the lighter.*

MAY. Give me a light.

AMY. They're mine, you didn't ask.

MAY. May I?

—

MAY *beckons for the lighter.* AMY *refuses.*

MAY *goes and lights her cigarette off the toaster, she lifts
her fringe up.*

Careful not to singe my fringe. Nate, you want one?

NATE. No thanks.

AMY. You don't smoke.

MAY. Nor do you, darling.

The two women glare – and inhale. Stand-off.

NATE. There's an Alpha Romeo in the drive.

MAY. What the hell is Tom doing here?

NATE. Who's Tom?

AMY. He's second-in-command to Mein Führer over there /

MAY. / Amy.

AMY. And he pretends that Mum scares him but secretly /

TOM *enters; briefcase – straight from the office – sees the two women smoking at each other – stands – confused.* AMY *doesn't see him.*

/ when she shouts he gets all sort of – (*A wimpish premature-ejaculation impression.*)

NATE. He's inside now.

AMY. Hi, Tom.

TOM. Amy.

NATE. Hi, I'm Nate.

TOM. And you are?

NATE. I'm her boyfriend.

TOM. Christ.

AMY. We'll go upstairs, won't we, Nate?

NATE. Oh yeah, wicked.

MAY. Stay next door where I can see you.

TOM *heads over to the TV and turns on the TV screen – he flicks through the channels until he gets to the news.*

AMY. You should work if you need to work.

NATE. Lovely to meet you, Mrs Singer, and you, man.

NATE offers TOM his hand – he doesn't take it; he's involved in the TV.

That's cool.

AMY goes for the packet of cigarettes on the island – MAY grabs them before she can get there and smiles.

AMY. They're mine; they're expensive.

MAY. So is dinner.

TOM turns up the volume – we hear a new article about the overthrow of King Idris by Colonel Gaddafi in the Libyan Revolution. The kids stop and stare at the screen – MAY stares at the screen. MAY looks at TOM, first time we've seen panic in decades – she takes a drag on the cigarette, looks out the window.

Shit.

NATE. Who is that?

TOM. Colonel Gaddafi.

MAY. Have they got to the wells?

AMY. You mean – is everyone okay?

TOM. The violence seems to be restricted to Tripoli but we got a telex from our head of HR at the drill site who said he could see tanks on the horizon.

MAY. Every day that that rig isn't making money we're still spending hundreds of thousands of pounds to have it just sit there.

AMY bangs a fork on the table.

Stop it, you're attention-seeking and it's aggravating.

TOM. Our men might die.

MAY. If they don't and we have to shut down then they'll all lose their jobs.

AMY *bangs a fork on the table*.

If you do that one more time. We need to work out the cost projections and be ready to talk to the board.

TOM. I've already spoken to the board.

MAY. Before coming here?

TOM. They were checking our situation.

MAY. And you said?

TOM. I'd come here and talk to you. They were emphatic about safeguarding production.

MAY. Why didn't they ring me?

AMY *bangs her fork on the table*.

MAY *snaps round to stare at* NATE. AMY *lifts the fork to bang it again –* MAY *stares at her*.

I said –

AMY. There's a man.

FAROUK. Mrs Singer.

MAY. How did you.

FAROUK. My name is Mr Farouk. I am the representative of Mr Gaddafi's Revolutionary Command Council currently conducting negotiations with the majors that are based in London. I hope you don't mind the intrusion, the door was open and time is of the essence.

Pause – no one responds.

I assume we're speaking English.

MAY. Sorry?

FAROUK. ؟إحناي ما نتكلّم بالعربي (*iḥnāy mā nitkallam bil 'arabī?*) [We aren't speaking in Arabic?]

TOM. Um – sorry, Mr Farouk, you're going to have to bear with us a moment we're playing catch u– /

MAY (*stepping in*). / It's lovely to meet you.

FAROUK. You're the fifth company I have spoken to this evening who operates in my country and has done for two decades and no one knows how to say hello.

TOM. *Salaam aleikum.*

FAROUK (*laughs slightly*). Yes.

AMY. *Masā' al-khayr, kayfa ḥālak?*

FAROUK. *Ana bekhair, shukran. Wa anti?*

AMY. *Muttaeb – ikn ana bekhair.*

MAY. What have I told you about speaking F… Just go upstairs, please.

AMY (*indicating* FAROUK). Us two?

MAY. No.

AMY. You sure you don't want me to translate?

MAY. Leave your bedroom door open please.

> AMY *and* NATE *take their supper and head for the door. They exit.*
>
> *Pause –* MAY, TOM *and* FAROUK *stand – stare at each other.*
>
> Mr Farouk, we have employees – and production – in the areas experiencing – turbulence.

FAROUK. Yes.

> *Odd beat.*

MAY. We'd like to be reassured that there's no cause for our employees to be nervous.

FAROUK. Yes. There is. Cause. To be Nervous.

MAY. Right.

FAROUK. The Declaratory Statement of Petroleum Policy recently adopted by OPEC member countries /

MAY. / There are so many of your OPEC resolutions it's hard
   to /

FAROUK. / was drawn up to help member countries, like
   ourselves, to exercise proper control over our own oilfields.
   To help us 'manage' the foreign companies that are operating
   on our land. Is this 'manage' – the right word? Forgive me if
   my English is /

MAY. / Your English is perfect.

FAROUK. Thank you.

TOM. Mr Farouk, I'm sure we've been operating within the
   terms of this Declaratory Statement; our lawyers are
   particularly vigilant about all OPEC resolutions.

FAROUK. I'm sure. Let me draw your attention to the points in
   question.

MAY. Please.

FAROUK. 'Where provision for Governmental participation in
   the ownership of the existing concession-holding company has
   not been made, the Government – may acquire a reasonable
   participation in the companies operating on our land.'

   Pause.

MAY. You wish to acquire participation in our company?

FAROUK. I'm so glad this is clear.

MAY. On what terms?

FAROUK. In the Declaratory Statement it says this is possible –
   'on the grounds of the principle of changing circumstances'.

MAY. The principle of changing circumstances?

FAROUK. You understand?

   MAY *breathes in ready to come back.*

TOM. May.

MAY. What degree of participation are you and the
   Revolutionary Command Council suggesting – exactly?

FAROUK. A twenty-five-per-cent ownership – or its financial equivalent.

MAY *laughs. There's riotous sexual giggling from* AMY *and* NATE *off –* MAY *stops laughing – looks up, livid.*

They're having a party?

MAY. I guess so.

FAROUK. That twenty-five-per-cent share will increase to fifty-one-per-cent – a majority share of your Libyan operation – in the next ten years.

A squeal of pleasure from upstairs.

MAY. Mr Farouk, these demands are perhaps to be expected of a new government that wants to see change. However, as our lawyers will make clear, these demands are entirely unrealistic.

FAROUK. We have enshrined this particular clause of the Declaratory Statement – in Libyan law.

TOM. I'm a bit scrappy on my Libyan law.

FAROUK. We have to understand British law so well for all the contracts, I presumed.

MAY. You can't just come and steal a quarter of a company that's been operating for twenty years.

FAROUK. It's not theft.

TOM. We'll sue.

FAROUK. Libyan law /

MAY. / International law /

FAROUK. / Under international law this is a conservation measure – we are conserving our resources.

MAY. Suddenly everyone's a conservationist.

FAROUK. Times are changing, Mrs Singer.

MAY. So it seems.

FAROUK. There could be something so feminine about you if only…

MAY. Times are changing, Mr Farouk.

TOM. Mr Farouk, thank you so much for taking the time to come and speak with us, we're going to need a few days to talk to people at our end and /

/ FAROUK *gets a contract out of his bag and puts it on the table.*

FAROUK. We'll need your signature accepting these contractual modifications – this evening.

TOM *and* MAY *stare at the piece of paper.* FAROUK *smiles.*

MAY. Or what?

TOM. May!

FAROUK. We are, of course, all interested in making sure that there is no disruption to supply.

MAY. If the British Government woke up tomorrow morning and marched into every French restaurant and Chinese takeaway and said apologies, L'escargot Bleu – terribly sorry, Oriental Kingdom – but we'll be taking a quarter from here on in. You'd think that was acceptable?

TOM. May.

FAROUK. Chinese food is not the world's most valuable resource, nor does it come out of the ground, Mrs Singer.

MAY. If Westminster reclaimed the air? Declared that a quarter of all soil suddenly belongs to the Government? And all businesses, including Libyan business, on that soil have to hand over a quarter of all revenue to the British Government? That would be fair?

FAROUK. It is a beautiful warm evening. The English is so balmy. You mind if I step outside to smoke? Give you a few minutes to consider your decision.

TOM. Of course.

FAROUK *exits*.

MAY. You get on the phone to every other major right now and we get an agreement across the board that the Revolutionary Command Council can go fuck itself.

TOM. It's gone six.

MAY. What?

TOM. They won't pick up their phones; they're at home with their families.

MAY. Why are you being so fucking useless.

TOM. We'll have to wait until tomorrow morning.

MAY *picks up the contract*.

MAY. We can't wait until tomorrow morning. They'll shut us down.

TOM. What do you want me to do?

MAY. Libya nationalises then what? Algeria? Kuwait? Iran? They cut us off, hospitals close, petrol queues miles long – kids won't be able to eat.

TOM. Don't be absurd.

MAY. In three days of a fuel crisis, supermarkets are empty. We don't have a spare twelve hours to cock about.

TOM. If we sign the deal, we safeguard supply and we keep our men safe. Easy.

MAY. And hand over a quarter of our profits? Without consulting the board?

TOM. If our hand was forced.

MAY. This isn't about our company, Tom. Whoever controls supply controls – everything.

TOM. Oh come on.

MAY. You're shaking.

TOM. What? No I'm not.

MAY. Your hand – it's shaking.

TOM. It's fine; I'm fine.

> AMY *and* NATE *enter*.

AMY. It's really hot in here – can we turn the heating down? I'm sweating like a pig.

MAY. Go back upstairs.

AMY. We're just going to get some ice cream.

> MAY *strides into the pantry gets a tub of ice cream – slams it on the table in front of* AMY.

Don't do that.

TOM. What?

AMY. Look at my legs just because I'm in a T-shirt. It's sick. I'm fifteen.

> AMY *takes a spoon of the ice cream – eats it, feeds a spoon to* NATE. *It is undeniably sexual.* MAY *catches sight of it.*

MAY. Will you use bowls please?

> AMY *moves to get the bowls –* NATE *grabs her round the waist on the way and kisses her neck.*

> MAY *puts two bowls on the counter.*

> AMY *stares at them both – hates the silence – spoons out the ice cream.*

Put it back in the freezer.

AMY. I'll do it in a minute.

MAY. Now, please.

AMY. We might want some more in a second.

MAY. You've had enough.

AMY. We can't know that until we've had this bit.

MAY. Put it back in the freezer.

AMY. It will be like two minutes, tops.

MAY. I said do it now.

AMY. Does it really matter if I do it now or in like /

MAY. / Yes, yes it matters because it's ice cream and it will melt. Please stop fighting me on every fucking corner, Amy!

TOM *grabs the ice cream off the side and marches to go and put it back in the freezer.*

AMY. Six months, the second I am sixteen and I am out of here like a shot. I'm dropping out of school and I'm moving in with Nate and when we have a family, which we will, my kids will be free from your fucking control-freakery – free to leave the ice cream for five fucking minutes and they will just have to face the consequences which are, incidentally, slightly melted ice cream! And by the way – we're fucking!

FAROUK *enters.*

MAY. I'm sorry, Mr Farouk, Tom hasn't quite yet had a chance to make the few phone calls that we wanted to make, if you could give us just five minutes more.

AMY *picks up her bowl and slams it on the table – hard – one, two, three.*

AMY *and* NATE *leave.*

FAROUK. If you're planning to ring the other companies I can save you the effort. They have all already signed.

MAY. I don't believe you.

FAROUK. Amoseas has been told to cut back production by two hundred thousand barrels a day, Oasis group told to cut back to a hundred and fifty from nine hundred, Mobil from two hundred and twenty to forty and they have all complied.

MAY. At some point, Mr Farouk, this stops being a corporate concern and becomes an issue of national security.

TOM. May!

FAROUK. Your Foreign Secretary is not going to stand against us.

MAY. Are you sure?

TOM. I don't think any of us need to be talking about national security, we've been working together peacefully for a long time – I'm sure there is a reasonable solution /

FAROUK. / Please, Mrs Singer – 'the day is far gone, let us take the necessary action before the night is at hand'.

FAROUK *slides the contract over to her*.

We'll take control by force, if necessary.

MAY. And that will be seen as an act of aggression against British nationals and our Foreign Secretary /

TOM. / Be careful.

NATE *enters*.

NATE. Amy was wondering if we could get some /

MAY. / Go back upstairs right now!

NATE *leaves*.

Where did you go to university, Mr Farouk?

FAROUK. Excuse me?

MAY. Did you understand the question?

FAROUK. LSE.

MAY. London. London School of Economics?

FAROUK. Yes.

MAY. And where do you send your engineers to train?

–

He doesn't respond.

Which country do you come to, to hire the engineers that work in the Libyan oil industry?

FAROUK. Oil is the product of our land.

MAY. Yes but your oil was explored, discovered, developed and transported using our equipment and our engineers.

FAROUK. You have been exploiting our soil for /

MAY. / That doesn't sound like exploitation to me – that sounds like guidance, instruction – that sounds like sharing expertise and information.

FAROUK. From which you have made a lot of money.

MAY. You've made a fair bit as well.

FAROUK. Not as much as you.

MAY. You would have been years behind where you are now if you'd been left to do it on your own. When we first came into your country you were begging us to set up shop. You gave me a ceremonial bowl.

FAROUK. And now we are taking back what's ours.

MAY. Yours?

FAROUK. It's under our ground.

MAY. When has land ever belonged to anyone for any other reason than someone marching in and taking it? The earth wasn't created with little dotted lines with scissor symbols all over it. It takes a hundred and fifty million years to make oil – Saudi Arabia has existed for forty years; the German Democratic Republic is only marginally older than my daughter – taking national boundaries too seriously in the distribution of global resources is short-sighted.

FAROUK. Well right now – under our Government – we declare it Libyan property and we will fight to see the end of Western companies operating in our country.

MAY. And we will fight to defend our right to be there.

FAROUK. It is not British land.

MAY. We inherited an empire. We are defending a superpower. I will not leave my child with less than I was given. I have worked too hard.

Pause.

FAROUK (*to* TOM). Do you have the capacity to go over her head? You can speak to the board?

—

TOM. I – I would have to talk to them in the morning. It would take some time.

MAY. Don't you dare.

FAROUK. I'd need your word now.

FAROUK *offers* TOM *his hand.*

TOM. I'm sorry my head it's going like the clappers – I can't um.

TOM *stares at* FAROUK*'s hand.*

FAROUK. Do you believe your country ever had a right to be drilling for oil in our country?

TOM. We're not a country – we're a company /

FAROUK. / A British company.

TOM. A commercial enterprise. Britain, as a country, is no longer in the Middle East.

FAROUK. Libya is not in the Middle East.

TOM. Sorry, I um – it was insensitive – I just meant /

FAROUK. / It's not insensitive, it's inaccurate. Libya is in North Africa.

TOM. I was using the example of Britain's recent withdrawal from Iran /

FAROUK. / Which is in a different continent to Libya. The distance between Tripoli and Tehran is probably greater than between London and Moscow.

TOM. What I was saying, Mr Farouk, is considering that we have just had our hands slapped and run out of Iran with our tail between our legs I can't see our company getting any support from our Government in resisting your demands. So our actions here are, purely, commercial.

FAROUK. You have the opportunity to do what you think is right and fair, you can be one of the good men in history.

TOM. Thank you.

FAROUK. Let me know when you have spoken to the board.

TOM *shakes* FAROUK*'s hand*.

Good evening.

TOM. Good evening.

FAROUK. *Wada'an*.

TOM. *Wada'an*.

FAROUK *exits*.

TOM *stares at* MAY, MAY *at* TOM.

What did you think you were going to do? Start a war?

MAY. War started the day we decided that we had a right to be warm even when the sun isn't shining.

TOM. We can afford to pay them their fair share.

NATE *enters*.

NATE *silently goes to the freezer to get ice cream*.

MAY. I'd like you to leave the house. Now.

NATE. What?

MAY. I need you to never see Amy again.

TOM. May?

MAY. One minute, Tom.

NATE. No.

MAY. No?

NATE. I don't want to do that.

MAY. I bet you don't. You're in the middle of fucking my daughter and eating ice cream, I can see why you wouldn't want to leave.

NATE. I want to talk to Amy.

MAY. Listen, Nate – I could stand here and tell you to have your fun, whilst your flesh is still clinging to your bones – before you look down in the shower and see that a hurricane has passed through. I can remember how skin can feel soft like summer, how staying up all night makes you the kind of tired that you wonder why anybody bothers sleeping. Right?

I could be tough and tell you that even if you go into it with fire you'll spend the rest of your life eking out a spark and eventually you'll resent her so much you won't have the stomach to look at yourself in the mirror.

I could even be cruel – and having seen your efforts on the kitchen table, inform you that you need to hone your craft, my friend, because there is no way on God's earth that I will allow my daughter the chafing and the precise knowledge of the pattern of her bedroom ceiling and most of all – the feeling of being desperately, repeatedly underwhelmed.

I will not let her spend the next three years trying to project heroism on to your average face. I will not watch her try to believe a god into you. You see, unlike you, she's determined – and she could get stuck on you and I won't let that happen.

It's my job to protect her future from the passions of her present.

–

NATE. She hates you – you know that?

MAY. No, she doesn't.

NATE. Yes, she does.

MAY. You don't shout at someone like that unless they've already got you by the tail. Does she ever shout at you like that?

Pause.

NATE. We love each other.

MAY. Of course you do, but that's not the point. Amy needs to get sharp on someone her own strength. You see, we're as sharp as the stone is strong that grinds us into shape… and you're a pebble from Surbiton.

Pause.

TOM. May?

NATE. You seem really lonely.

Pause.

MAY. Do I?

NATE. Yes. I don't think you're a very good mother.

MAY. I don't think – what with you being a sixteen-year-old boy – that you know shit about it.

–

NATE. You know being smart isn't as good as being happy.

Pause – MAY looks at NATE, as if she might reconsider.

She's not as great as you think she is.

MAY. And there it is, as I suspected. It's time for you to leave.

Pause – NATE looks at MAY – challenges her for a moment.

You haven't got the fight in you.

NATE *picks up his beer and exits.*

And you just proved it.

The front door slams.

MAY *takes a breath, takes a swig of her drink.* MAY *turns on* TOM.

You should get some sleep, Tom – you've got a coup to stage.

TOM. You'll lose her doing things like that.

MAY. We'll see.

TOM *picks up his briefcase and turns to go.*

That's it, is it?

TOM *stops.*

I'll just wait for a knock on my office door in the morning? Some secretary sent to tell me to pack my things because none of the big boys in suits had the balls?

MAY *starts taking out the ingredients for and making hot chocolate.*

TOM. If it's for Amy – surely keeping your income means more than standing your ground on this?

MAY. Your kids spend the holidays in your wife's big family house. You have never feared that your children might ever fall back down through the cracks. There's still blood on my hands from hauling myself up, from clinging on.

TOM. And because you've worked for it you're excused from ever thinking about anyone other than yourself?

MAY. Amy.

TOM. That's going to stop working soon, May. You've done your job there – you're going to need to come up with a better excuse.

—

I'm going to get home in time to kiss my kids goodnight for the first time this week.

MAY. And what are you going to put in your car to get you there?

TOM *exits*.

AMY *enters*.

AMY. Nate broke up with me.

MAY. Oh, love. I'm so sorry.

AMY stares at her mother, confused by her sincerity.

AMY. Do you love me?

MAY. More than you could possibly imagine. This will be the making of you. I promise.

AMY throws the mug of hot chocolate, full pelt, at MAY. MAY swerves successfully – but the chocolate flies – and lands thick over the top of the white counter.

AMY. You asked him to leave! Just because you're on your own – just because you're some sad old hag that drove away whichever unfortunate unknown man that created me – doesn't mean I have to be!

—

MAY. I'm sorry that you're hurting.

AMY. Ring him and make him come back.

MAY. You ring him and make him come back. (*Beat*.) Or have you already tried that? Is that why you're angry?

AMY. He's probably terrified.

MAY. Do you really want to be with someone that leaves you because your mother told them to?

Long pause.

AMY. I wish you would leave.

AMY shoves MAY. MAY doesn't move.

MAY. And yet here I am. He thinks infrastructure is a kind of light ray!

AMY. That doesn't mean we couldn't make a happy family.

Pause.

MAY. If you loved you – like I love you. You would not let you fuck him. If you loved you like I love you – you wouldn't smoke show-off cigarettes, you wouldn't pluck your eyebrows until it looked like an ant had pissed across your forehead. I love you more than you love you right now – and that is why I know what's best. I won't let some boy be the end of you. You will do more than love a man. I swear to God, I will not let love take your knees out. You can have it when you're done with the important stuff.

AMY. And what if I never fall in love again? What if I'm Prime Minister but I never fall in love again?

MAY. If you're asking me to choose between you being Prime Minister and you fucking Nate for the rest of your life you might need to pick a harder question.

AMY. He made me happy.

MAY. Life is long and love doesn't always last.

AMY. Doesn't it? Then why have I seen you standing down here in the middle of the night, staring into the garden with tears running down your face?

MAY *breathes in deep – recovers enough…*

MAY. I'm sorry he wasn't better. I do understand how hard that is – how painful and disappointing and hard and – exhausting it is that he wasn't better.

AMY *sobs and sobs and dissolves into a heap on the floor.*

AMY. He's not going to come back, is he? He won't fight for me, will he?

MAY. I'd be surprised.

AMY *stands, dazed – irrevocably wounded. Exits.*

MAY *doesn't move – stares at the way her daughter went.*

MAY *stands,* MAY *stares.*

MAY *lights a cigarette, takes a drag.*

MAY *stands*. MAY *fills up her drink*. MAY *goes to drink it –
her hand shakes*. MAY *looks out across the dark of the
garden. She stares, exhausted*. MAY *starts to clean the hot
chocolate off the top of the counter – she can't seem to get
rid of it – even though she's trying – trying and trying – she's
so tired of trying – she works at it – works and works but it
just won't go… so –* JOSS.

JOSS. I knew a girl who liked to roar.
    Howl herself hoarse.
    Had to lay her down and get her sated.
    Only way wild could find its peace.

    —

    What is this place, babe? Listen to that hum. (*Winces*.)
    Fucking – tinny – thin, nothing sort of place, this.

    —

    What were you so scared of?

    —

    Of mud? Of cold? Of kicking the bow of a tree till your foot
    bones break? Blood? Scratching at each other till there's
    flesh under your nails?

    I know how you smell.

He inhales – deep – he exhales. MAY *closes her eyes – the
wanting of him is almost too much.*

    I bet you've fucked some frogs to try and cure yourself of
    me. I bet you fucked some spineless fucking idiots to try and
    disappoint yourself back to sanity.

MAY *turns to him, puts the palm of her hand over his face.*

JOSS *takes the hand at the wrist – sniff the palm – kisses it.*

    Try and turn your blood tepid but you can't.

JOSS *takes her palm and places it flat against his chest – she
can feel his heartbeat – so strong – it's the river that runs in
her – it's too much and she can't bear it.*

Tch. There it is.

MAY *can hardly breathe*.

That's what you've been running from.

MAY *tries to pull her hand away, turn away*.

MAY. I have a child. I had no choice.

—

JOSS. She's not just yours.

MAY. I – I – you need to leave.

JOSS *roams around the kitchen – picking things over – he sees a picture of* AMY *on the fridge*.

JOSS (*stops suddenly, choked up with pride*). Is that her?

MAY *can't – tries to breathe – looks away*.

MAY *nods – tiny*.

She's pretty. (*Laughs*.) She's got your wild in her eyes.

JOSS *shakes his head*.

MAY. This is my home – and I'm telling you to leave.

JOSS. On whose land? On whose soil?

MAY. I bought it, I worked for it – I've kept a lid on all… and you're right – there's no life in it – no blood – no – (*Puts her palm on her own chest*.) – nothing.

—

JOSS. You said you'd die without me.

MAY. I have died.

—

JOSS *stands and stares at her*.

JOSS. You're a beast and it's going to waste.

JOSS *picks her up, no problem at all and carries her over to the counter. He sits her up on it like a child. He kisses her, hard.* MAY*'s knees go, she crumbles entirely.* MAY *inhales – deep – it's mud, it's ground, it's soil – it's nothing we've seen for centuries.* MAY *kisses him again – it's almost feral – she wants him, she misses him, she's desperate to go back to where she began. He dissolves from between her hands – he disappears into the sink – and down into the plughole – and the chocolate, mud – the soil with it. The kitchen hums with sterility – there is no life in it – the zingy-tingyness of over-lit, over-heated, over-processed materialism.* MAY *stares –* JOSS *is gone.* MAY *crumbles, devastated.*

MAY *picks herself up – mops up – cleans – sprays – it is all shining white.* MAY *pours herself a gin and tonic, her hand shakes slightly – she takes one of* AMY*'s cigarettes out of the packet and tries to light it. She shakes. She stands.*

Pause.

AMY. Everybody's gone.

MAY. I'm still here.

AMY. I can't find my netball socks and I need them for tomorrow morning.

MAY. They're in the washing basket.

AMY *gets them out.*

AMY. They're dirty.

MAY. That'll be because they've been on your feet.

AMY. Aren't there any clean ones?

MAY. You can borrow mine; they're in my sock drawer.

AMY. I want the long ones though – if I wear the short ones I look like a prick.

MAY. That might just be the sacrifice you have to make, darling.

Small pause. MAY *comes behind* AMY – *holds her.*

You're shaking.

AMY. I saw from my bedroom window.

MAY *goes over to the window – looks out.*

MAY. What?

AMY. There was a man. He was burning.

MAY. Where?

AMY. He was kneeling on the pavement – out on the street, with his forehead pressed against the side of the car. He looked like he was praying to the car. When he lifted his head back I could see he had this tube in his mouth and the other end was in the bit where you put the petrol.

He went up like a bonfire.

MAY. There's nothing there.

AMY. He couldn't stop the flames.

MAY. There's nothing there.

AMY. My pyjamas are all wet with sweat.

MAY. You see a straight line stretching from here – from where you are now – can you see – you – on the horizon, she's travelled so far, she's doing incredible things in the world – look at her, can you see her? She's looking back at you – she's smiling – she's saying 'it's going to be okay' – 'it's going to be better than you can possibly imagine'.

Small pause.

Can you see her? Come on, you've got school in the morning.

MAY *exits.* AMY *is left alone in the kitchen.*

AMY *looks at the table full of the food from dinner. She opens the cupboards, she opens the fridge – she finds all the food she can and she scoffs and scoffs and scoffs – she can't help but stuff it in her face with panic.*

MAY *stands in the doorway; unseen by* AMY *– and watches her scoff.*

Interval.

Interscene

A woman flies across a desert.
She flies and flies and flies and flies.

Toddlers are shot in the back
By planes with no pilots in them.

She asks the hostess for extra ice.
She flies above time.

86

PART FOUR

Desert, nr. Kirkuk, Kurdistan – 2021

Desert – outside Baghdad, direction of Kirkuk.

A burning red sun is low in the sky. These are the dog days. The heat makes the horizon bend. A car drives across a desert. Sand flies.

AMINAH gets out. AMY gets out, AMY looks about, there's desert for miles and miles.

AMINAH leans back against the car, lights a cigarette.

AMY. شي بخبّل. (*shī bikhabbil.*) [It's fucking nuts.]

AMINAH. تريدين سيجارة؟ (*trīdīn sijāra?*) [You want a cigarette?]

AMY. لا، آني تمام. (*lā, āni tamām.*) [No, I'm fine.]

> *AMY stands and looks at the desert – breathes it in.*
>
> *The women stand and look at the space.*
>
> كنتي تيجين هنا وإنتي صغيرة؟ (*kunti tījīn-hna winti sghīra?*) [You used to come here as a kid?]

AMINAH. إيه طبعاً. زين، مو بالله؟ (*ēh tab'an. zien, mūballah?*) [Sure. It's nice, right?]

> *AMINAH takes out her phone and checks something on it – whilst AMY looks out, drinking it in.*

AMY. وأكيد النجوم بالليل. (*wakīd lenjūm billēl.*) [I bet the stars at night...]

AMINAH. إيه. (*ēh.*) [Yeah.]

> *AMY grabs AMINAH and pulls her away from the car, she almost stumbles the phone and there's an odd desperation to not dropping it.*

لا لا، دخيلك - عندي صداع كحول. بالله وقفي. (*lā lā dakhīlik – 'indi sudā' kuḥūl. ballahi wagfi.*) [Hey come on, no – don't – I'm hungover. No – man, stop it.]

AMY. إنتي اللي جبتيني لهنا. (*intilli jibtīni lihna.*) [You bought me here.]

AMINAH. قلتي تريدين فسحة. (*gilti trīdīn fusḥa.*) [You said you wanted space.]

AMY *stands* AMINAH *in front of the desert – makes her look.*

(*Laughs, wriggles out of* AMY*'s grip*). هاذي صحرا. (*hādhi saḥra.*) [It's a desert.]

AMY. فراغ. تموتين بيوم إذا حاولتي تمشين بيه. (*farāgh. tmūtīn byōm idha ḥāwalti timshīn bīh.*) [Nothingness. You'd be dead in a day if you tried to walk it.]

AMINAH. أظن يومين أو ثلاثة. (*adhunn yōmēn aw thlātha.*) [Two or three, I reckon.]

AMY. تحسّين بإنّك كلّش صغيرة. (*tḥissīn b'innik kullish sghīra.*) [It makes you feel so – small.]

AMINAH*'s phone rings, it's a cheesy Iraqi pop song.*

هاذا مو زين. الله يقطع الغنية هاذي من هنا. (*hādha mū zien. alla yigta' el-ghinya hādhi min-hna.*) [That's wrong. That shouldn't be here, that fucking song should not be here.]

AMINAH *picks up the phone.*

AMINAH. إيه. إيه. (*ēh. ēh.*) [Yes. Yes.]

AMINAH *puts the phone down, starts walking to the car.*

AMY. منو؟ (*manū?*) [Who?]

AMINAH *leans inside the car, turns on music in the car – she chooses the same song, turns it up really loud.* AMINAH *starts dancing – grabs* AMY*, wants her to dance with her – the space of the desert, the sky – it's wild and weird, oddly performative.*

شبيكي؟ (*shbīki?*) [What's wrong with you?]

AMINAH *sings the song – tries to get* AMY *to join in,*
AMY *finds it odd.*

The sound of a car.

أكو سيارة. (*aku sayyara.*) [There's a car.]

AMINAH *keeps dancing.*

أمينة؟ (*Aminah?*) [Aminah?]

AMINAH *tries to ignore it –* AMY *grabs her and makes
her look.*

أكو حد جاي. (*aku ḥadd jāy.*) [Someone's coming.]

AMINAH. لا تخافين. (*la tkhāfīn.*) [Don't worry about it.]

—

AMY *stands off – stares at* AMINAH.

AMY. هم جايين لهنا. أمينة؟ أمينة؟ (*hum jāyyīn lihna. AMINAH?
AMINAH?*) [They're coming here. Aminah? Aminah?]

AMY *starts to panic, grabs* AMINAH, *drags her back
toward the car.* AMINAH *stands, doesn't move – doesn't go
with* AMY.

أعطيني المفتاح! أمينة؟ (*a'tīni el-miftāḥ! Aminah?*) [Give me the
keys! Aminah?]

The car pulls up – doors slam. AMY *stands.* AMINAH
stands.

MAY *enters, high status.*

Mum!

Long pause.

AMY *looks from* MAY *to* AMINAH.

MAY. Love?

MAY *holds her arms open to* AMY.

AMY. What are you doing here?

MAY. Aminah helped me find you.

AMY. تدرين؟ إنتي كنتي تدرين؟ (*tidrīn? inti kunti tidrīn?*) [You knew? You knew about this?]

AMINAH. هاذي أمك. (*hādhi ummik.*) [She's your mother.]

MAY. Don't shout at her.

> AMY *steps back – snatches the keys from* AMINAH *and makes for the car.*

> Amy. I want you home.

AMY. I'm not a child – you cannot just turn up and /

MAY. / You wouldn't respond to any of the messages I /

AMY. / I'm here. I belong here.

MAY. You don't.

AMY. You don't get to tell me where I belong. (*To* AMINAH.) جينا لهنا نتفرّج عالصحرا؟ (*jīna lihna nitfarraj 'as-sahra?*) [We came out here to look at the desert?]

AMINAH. هاذي أمك. (*hādhi ummik.*) [She's your mother.]

AMY. هاذي مو أمي. لازم نرجع للمستشفى - رح تسوقين؟ (*hādhi mū ummi. lāzim nirja' lil-mustashfa – rah tsūgīn?*) [She's not my mother. We need to get back to the hospital – are you going to drive?]

AMINAH. إسمعي لأمك. (*isma'ī la-ummik.*) [Listen to her.]

MAY. I brought you some chicken sandwiches. They're your favourite – I thought you might want something that reminded you of home.

AMY. I'm fine thanks.

AMINAH. Listen to her.

AMY. You don't speak English.

AMINAH. Sure I do.

AMY. We never speak English.

AMINAH *shrugs*.

You know what she is?

AMINAH. She's your mother.

AMY. No. She's an MP –

MAY. Ex-MP.

AMY. That voted for this – for the bomb that /

/ MAY *opens her jacket – to reach inside it*. MAY *takes out an envelope – takes out a wodge of cash – counts it – hands it to* AMINAH. AMY *stands shell-shocked*.

MAY. Thank you. You can leave us.

AMINAH (*to* AMY). Can I have the keys?

AMY. You can look me in the face and ask for them, no?

AMINAH. She's your mother.

AMY. I stayed awake with you when you were too scared to sleep.

AMINAH. Give me my money.

AMY. How much?

AMINAH *shrugs*.

How much is in the envelope?

AMINAH. I need to rebuild my house.

AMINAH *reaches for the keys*, AMY *snatches them away from her – she's not having them*.

MAY. Amy?

AMY (*to* MAY). You're not humanitarian. You've had to cross through territory that /

MAY. / Why don't you get in my car and we can discuss it on the way to the airport?

AMY. I'd like to know why you haven't been put in the back of a truck and had your fucking head chopped off because I can guarantee you they know that you're here.

MAY. Get in the car.

AMY. What deal did you cut?

MAY. Just get in the car, Amy.

AMY. I want to know why they're not touching you.

—

—

AMY *stares at her mother – searching her face – smiles, slowly – it dawns on her.*

MAY. There are women throwing their children on to sinking ships to get them out of here and you come here by choice?

AMY. To atone for the sins of my mother.

MAY. And it makes you feel good. It makes you feel necessary and brave and alive.

AMY. What's the deal?

MAY. I want you home.

AMY. You stood up in Parliament, in front of a country and said that you refused to accept the moral depravity of terrorists. Now you're making deals with them?

MAY. To keep you safe.

AMY. I've been fine for three years. It's you that needs protection.

MAY. To take you home.

AMY. You didn't need to come.

MAY. You think they don't know who you are?

AMY. I've been fine.

MAY. They've been biding their time.

AMY. They're not really time-biders, Mum.

MAY. If you hadn't put yourself in harm's way then /

AMY. / Whatever you have done – you have not done it in my name. Be very sure about that.

MAY. Of course I have! I've never done anything for any other reason.

AMY. I don't believe you.

MAY. When you were a baby, I'd watch you sleep – you'd snuggle right up into the top corner of your crib – you'd pull your teddy in behind you like a barricade. I swore, I swore I'd always keep you safe.

AMY. But it's not just that, is it?

MAY. Give Aminah the keys and get in my car.

AMY. No.

MAY. Get in the car!

AMY. What have you got that would do them more good than kidnapping you?

MAY. Amy.

AMY. How about you tell the truth for once in your life,

—

MAY. We've set up an offshore company that will provide the infrastructure necessary for the export of oil out of this region on to the world market.

—

AMINAH. ما أفهم. (*mā afham*.) [I don't understand.]

MAY. The Iraqi territory that they control is currently producing around fifty thousand barrels a day; it could be producing six times that.

AMY. And you want to help them reach their potential?

MAY. The world is no longer in a position to leave one of its biggest oil fields untapped; no matter who happens to be occupying it.

AMY. Oh we *need* it, do we? No matter what it costs we *need* it?

MAY. Our only sense of how much oil there is left in the world is how much they tell us there is. And the more they say they have, the more we allow them to sell. So we have no idea. We have never really had any idea. We've had to take them at their word.

AMY. Gulf War 1990, sanctions that killed hundreds of thousands of children, Operation Desert Fox 1998, 2001 we bomb them again, 2003 Iraq War, 2018 second Iraq War – You have devastated this country over and over and over again and you still don't have what you want.

MAY. It's running out.

AMY. It's always been running out.

MAY. We need /

AMY. / So you take.

MAY. It's only going to get worse. You need to come home.

> AMY *rips the envelope of cash out of* AMINAH's *hand.*

AMY (*to* AMINAH). تدرين من وين الفلوس هاذي؟ (*tidrīn min wē li-flūs hādhi?*) [Do you know where that money is from?]

AMINAH. Give me the money.

AMY. It's dirty.

AMINAH. I need it.

AMY. Do you know what she's done?

MAY. If we didn't do the deal someone else would have. It would have been the Russians or the Chinese. Now, get in the car. I'm taking you home.

AMY. أمينة؟ تفهمين؟ (*Aminah? tifhamīn?*) [Aminah? Do you understand?]

AMINAH. Go home.

AMY. What?

AMINAH. This isn't your country – go home.

AMY. Are your kids going to thank you for /

AMINAH. / Eventually a country gets rich enough and brutality gets replaced by nice cars and new trainers.

MAY. She has a family to think about.

AMINAH. My mother is sick.

MAY. She has responsibilities.

AMINAH. Give me my money.

> AMY *looks at the envelope of cash*.

AMY. There's hardly anything in here.

AMINAH. Give it to me.

AMY. Aminah?

AMINAH. You want to save my soul? Hm? Is that it, Amy?
You stood in front of a desert and you said it makes you feel humble. It takes a whole fucking desert, does it? I have to take the gas out of my car and put it in the generator so my mother has enough light to eat. In your country you keep the lights on all day from our oil and you don't even have the decency to sit under them, you come here. You think I don't speak English? You were so keen to use your Arabic you never asked.

AMY. I –

AMINAH. You think we're all illiterate and on our knees with our long suffering? When you drop your bombs –

AMY. They're not mine.

AMINAH. – When *your* country drops its bombs – it is briefcases that get thrown in the air. My father was on his way to work. I am a qualified engineer. I am working cleaning shit in a hospital. It takes a desert to make you feel humble? You come here to feel humble? So you can feel the pain of my people? Do you? You feel it? Because you stay awake all night when I am nearly dead?

AMY. I stayed awake because you're my friend. I didn't want you to be scared.

AMINAH. I have to go. I need to give my mother her supper. There is no one else to look after her.

AMY. You can't just accept the /

AMINAH. / Give me my keys.

AMY. الشعب يريد إسقاط النظام. (Ash-shab yurid isqat an-nizam.)

AMINAH. Everyone else got rid of their leaders – but we needed your help, didn't we?

AMY. You have to fight.

AMINAH. There has been war in my country as long as I've been alive. She lets them sell the oil – maybe it will run out quicker and at last we can have some peace.

AMINAH *takes the keys out of* AMY*'s hand.*

AMY. This deal legitimises them.

AMINAH. Are you going to give me my money? Or are you going to make me beg?

AMY *gives* AMINAH *the money.*

AMY. Don't leave me here; I don't want to get in the car with her. Don't make me do that, Aminah? Please.

AMINAH. She's your mother. She's offering you help. Grow up. Go home.

AMINAH *gets back into the car, we hear the music blast.*

AMINAH *exits.*

MAY. If you hate what I do? Take over, make better choices. Stop being angry at the generation in power, become the generation in power. It can't be someone else's fault forever.

AMY. I'm not coming back.

—

MAY. You're going to miss it – one day you're going to wake up and it's going to be too late.

AMY. What?

MAY. You're never going to find a man that matches how this makes you feel.

AMY. I – I'm /

MAY. / Have you loved anyone more than him since?

AMY. What?

MAY. Have you?

AMY. No but that doesn't mean I loved him enough.

MAY. Your expectations are – at some point you have to return to real life. Tedious conversation. Compromise. Responsibility /

AMY. / You don't think I have responsibility /

MAY. / Not the kind the scares you, no. This is other people. You can give them everything because you don't owe them anything.

AMY. And what do I owe you?

MAY. You need to come home. You should have a family. Settle down.

AMY. For you or for me?

MAY. You have no idea what life is like for a woman that is over fifty and on her own.

AMY. You have spent my entire life telling me I should never settle for anything less than the best. To believe I deserved /

MAY. / I was wrong.

AMY. What?

MAY. I thought the world would be different – I thought men would be better by the time you grew up – I thought you could hold on to your power as you got older – I thought I'd always have choices, I was wrong. Men go out with women twenty years younger, you get retired from life without asking, women that felt like allies defect to husbands and grandchildren. I know so many brilliant women that have ended up alone. They could not yield; they were too strong.

AMY. What? Too strong, that's not possible. /

MAY. / They are brilliant and lonely. It's excruciating, trust me. I don't want that for you.

AMY. You told me to be everything that I can be! You told me to never compromise! You promised me that hard work, that progress was the answer.

MAY. I was wrong. I wish I'd learnt to ask for less earlier. I'm sorry.

AMY. You're sorry?

MAY. If you had children you wouldn't be here.

AMY. Well I don't.

MAY. You wouldn't be here because you would realise that there are more important things.

AMY. I belong here. I'm doing good work.

MAY. You're hiding.

AMY. Nope.

MAY (*taking a step toward* AMY). What are you so scared of? What are you running from? You can't live without love, no one can.

AMY. I love what I do.

MAY. Come home. Come home with your mum.

AMY. I can't.

MAY. Can't what?

AMY. People here, Aminah's family – they sleep in the same room. Five, ten – all close together. I can't do that. I couldn't even. When I was. The flat, his clothes on the floor, going to bed in the same way with the same person, having the same conversation every fucking night; I can't do it. There was one night – I couldn't sleep – I looked at him sleeping, the sound of him breathing, that whistle – the relentlessness, on and on and on – I wanted to put a pillow over his face to make it stop, so furious with wanting my own space.

At about 4 a.m. – I was standing by the window, desperately waiting for the sky to get light. I put my shoes on and walked – just walked – the streets with houses all asleep, empty shops, empty stations; I stood on Waterloo Bridge at dawn and looked. (*Takes a deep breath – tries to catch her breath.*)

The size of it. How well it all worked – everything I could see only existed because someone once imagined it might be possible.

She laughs.

I got a room in a hotel. I lay down on the bed and I could breathe for the first time in. I stared at the ceiling and thought of all the women in the world that were lying in bed alone. I could see us – like little tin soldiers, each in our ocean of white sheet – cool and calm and on our own, in our twenties and thirties, forties, fifties sixties and seventies – across the world – like a silent army. It felt – so – obvious, so exciting, our quiet secret – that we all know – we were made to be alone.

I slept better than I'd slept for years.

I woke up. Ordered myself a boiled egg; good bread, salty butter – heavy silver knife, thick linen. Newspaper. Strong coffee. (*Smiles, laughs softly.*) I was happy.

MAY. It's freedom.

AMY. Yes.

MAY. It's not love.

AMY. It feels like love – without the trap.

MAY. You're alone.

AMY. But alive.

MAY. That's the trap.

> MAY *turns to go back to the car* – AMY *stands and watches her go.*

> I'm sorry if it was something I did that made you this way. I thought I was doing the best /

AMY. / I'm fine.

MAY. You have such a huge capacity for love I can't bear to see it go to waste.

AMY. You should go.

MAY. You just have to be brave enough to try.

AMY. Brave? Me? I feel big here. I feel like I'm being everything that I can be. I'm brilliant here.

MAY. Look after yourself.

> MAY *turns to leave.*

AMY. Mum?

MAY. Hm.

AMY. I need a lift back to town.

> *Helicopter blades – sand flies – up it goes and breakfast.*

> AMY *sits down at an exceptionally well-made breakfast table. She's a mess – she's covered in blood – she's exhausted – she hasn't slept in days. She is served by an Iraqi man in white tie – she has coffee – tea, a beautiful little boiled egg with toast.*

Can I get some extra butter? And some salt? Thank you.

> *The butter arrives – and the salt* – AMY *makes herself the perfect mouthful.*

AMY *opens the paper.*

AMY *has the mouthful – follows it with a mouthful of coffee – smiles – turns the page of the paper over – she reads, she smiles.*

As she puts the cup back on the saucer her hand shakes slightly.

Interscene

A child flies backwards into the future.

A child drives backwards.
A child walks backwards

Retreats, returns, retracts
Yestermorrow.

A child returns, retreats, contracts
A child sits.

Home in time for bed.

PART FIVE

Farm, Cornwall – 2051

The Singer Farm.

Bare interior. Grey light. Dead screens. Dead lights. Dead consoles.

Windows – nothing but grey light.

Snow outside, piled high.

Two armchairs.

AMY *and* MAY *sit. Older, heavier.*

MAY. You've got more than I have.

AMY. No I haven't.

MAY. You have.

AMY. You did the portions.

MAY. You did the portions.

AMY. You know you did the portions. Stop it.

MAY. Stop it.

AMY. Stop it.

MAY. Stop it.

AMY. Stop it.

MAY. You stop it.

AMY. It's cold.

MAY. It's meant to be hot.

AMY. I meant the – air – the – not the soup.

MAY. It's snowing.

AMY. I know it's snowing.

MAY. So why say it's cold?

AMY. Why are you in such a stupid mood?

MAY. Why are you in such a stupid mood?

AMY. You've got toothpaste on your face.

MAY. Are there potatoes in this?

AMY. You made it.

MAY. Give me one of your potatoes.

AMY. Have it – go on just have it. Have all of it.

> AMY *puts her bowl on her mother's tray.*

MAY. Don't be daft.

AMY. I don't want it.

MAY. Don't be a silly willy.

AMY. I said I don't want it. Just have it. If you want it just have all of it.

MAY. Bath time?

AMY. No bath.

> MAY *sings the eighth line of the pre-chorus of 'Love Yourself' by Justin Bieber, beginning 'My mama don't like you...'*

Stop it.

> MAY *sings the next line.*

Stop it.

> *And then the next.*

Stop it.

> *They stare at each other a moment – they can't stop from smiling – it's one of* AMY*'s favourites.*

AMY *bellows the last line of the pre-chorus and then they both sing out the first two lines of the chorus,*

They both burst out laughing– it's fun.

I hate that old shit.

MAY. Makes an old girl happy. I remember listening to that when I was driving.

AMY (*collapses back in her chair*). UGGHHH. Please no. 'When I was young we had to make our own.' 'When I was young we had to go and get things from the shops and bring it back.'

MAY. You don't know you're born.

AMY. It'd be hard to ignore it – you're sitting right fucking there.

MAY. I'm going to run a bath.

AMY. Don't.

MAY. Bubbles. Oils. The old stuff. Glass of wine. So hot it stings but it makes all your flesh let go like it's got no choice and it leaves you all ruddy after.

AMY. Please don't turn the override on.

MAY. There's no devil in you.

AMY. Tin man.

MAY. I'm going to turn it on.

AMY. Restrain yourself.

MAY *lifts up the device and is about to click it into action – she threatens over the button.*

You can have a hot bath now or or we can afford to charge the car.

MAY *hovers over the button.*

I don't want to be stuck.

MAY. I've given you hot baths your whole life.

AMY. And you had one straight after.

MAY. I deserve one I'm old.

AMY. I'm old.

MAY. I've worked.

AMY. I've worked.

AMY. I'll hug you.

MAY. What?

AMY. If you're cold – I'll hug you. The way you like. I'll hug you if you don't turn the override on.

MAY. We could get some bread and cheese and set up in here. Just us two. A little team. There's some chicken in the fridge.

AMY. Fridge has gone warm.

AMY stares – doesn't move.

MAY. I'll save my hug. Put it in my back pocket. For later.

AMY. That's fine.

They both stare out of the window – there's nothing else to do.

Do you remember horizon?

MAY. What?

AMY. On a boat. Or across a field, on a long walk – or sometimes, even in a city you'd walk round a corner and by total surprise – the wide of it – with the – line and the – bigness in your eyes. It sort of.

AMY puts her hand in the middle of her own chest – the JOSS way.

MAY. What made you think of that?

AMY. Don't know. I just.

MAY. Breathe in.

AMY. Don't feel like playing.

MAY. Why not?

AMY. –

MAY. Get it up on Baidu.

AMY. What?

MAY. Get a picture of one up on Baidu. Baidu horizon. I think you're wrong.

AMY. Wrong?

MAY. I don't think it's the right word for what you described.

AMY. What is the right word?

MAY. It's mist or pink or dawn or something – get it up on Baidu.

AMY. I can't. We're in a black patch.

MAY. Sorry. I forgot for a second.

AMY. It is the right word.

MAY. We can't know now, can we.

AMY. We can know because I said so and I said that I know I'm right.

MAY. You're wrong.

AMY. I'm not wrong.

MAY. I know, darling, but I think you are.

AMY. But I'm not. Because it's my head. It's what I can see in my head /

MAY. / I know, darling, but the word.

AMY. I can see it. I can see it in my head and I can feel it in my – (*Slaps her chest.*)

MAY. But the word.

AMY. You must know that you're not completely right because you are, in fact, wrong. You can't just deliver everything like you know you're right, like you believe in your bones that you're right. You can't do that! Not when there are only two of us in here!

MAY. Baidu it!

AMY. We can't – black patch.

MAY. Don't shout at me.

AMY. We're in a black patch.

MAY. Don't shout at me!

AMY. We're in a fucking black patch!

MAY. Because you won't let us switch the emergency override on.

AMY. We can't afford the emergency override.

MAY. We'll be fine.

AMY. You always say that.

MAY. And here we are.

Pause – AMY *stares at her mother.*

Roof over our head, food in our stomachs.

—

AMY. If I'd kept my job I could have paid it.

MAY. Don't say it like you left for me. You couldn't afford to live alone.

AMY. I could share.

MAY. You hated sharing.

AMY. I might be better at it now.

MAY. At your age?

AMY. A change is as good as a rest.

MAY. You'd rather live with a stranger than with your own
    mother?

    —

    I'd understand – if you had a husband or a boyfriend or
    children.

    —

    Come here, you've got a bit of hair that's just /

AMY. / It's fine.

MAY. Come here, I'll tuck it.

AMY. Leave it, it's fine.

MAY. May.

AMY. I'm Amy.

MAY. I said Amy.

AMY. You said May.

MAY. I meant Amy.

AMY. Was there a burning man?

MAY. What?

    —

    —

AMY. When I was little I saw this. I used to dream. I saw
    a burning man.

MAY. It was a dream.

AMY. It doesn't feel like a dream. I looked at him and then
    I looked at you and I remember you blinking. People don't
    blink in dreams.

MAY. I don't know who you're talking about.

AMY. Okay.

MAY. Amy.

AMY. No, it's okay.

MAY. Amy?

AMY. No, it's fine.

MAY. Hey, darling girl – love, hey hey. Come back. Come here.

AMY hasn't moved, she's sitting right there.

AMY. Why can't you tell me? What are you so scared of?

They stare at each other – it might be possible for a moment.

They both breathe in – they breathe in further and further like it might be enough to kill them – they really go for it – it's odd – dangerous somehow – and then… they play the breathing-out game – one long noise – squeaky and high for one – low and rumbling for the other, they go and go and go and then it dies – there is silence – real silence.

AMY thumps on the floor three times. Nothing happens for some time.

AMY stares.

Crunching steps from outside.

The braying of a horse.

The horse comes closer over the crunching of the snow.

The horse walks past the window.

The horse's breath is hot on the window.

The horse stops outside.

JOSS, bulky, enters. He's carrying bags full of things, there's something Mother Courage about him – we feel like he's been travelling for years.

JOSS. Sorry to interrupt.

MAY and AMY look at JOSS. Then they look at each other.

You got any fire? Can't feel my fingers.

AMY. Fire?

JOSS. No?

AMY. No.

    –

    Did you come on a horse?

JOSS. Easiest thing in the snow.

MAY. Hello.

JOSS. Hi there.

    MAY *steps forward to touch his face.* JOSS *sort of laughs
    awkwardly and steps back from her.*

    What you doing?

MAY. Sorry.

AMY. Are you selling something?

JOSS. I'm looking for motors. Anything that has a motor in it –
    electric fans, food processors. Anything that goes round and
    round.

AMY. We don't use them any more, scratch-make does our
    chopping. Tesco-Sainsbury but it's all wired in.

JOSS. I'd pay you for 'em, obviously. Old drone propellors?
    You run 'em backwards and they make generators, see.

    JOSS *takes out a motor that is connected to a tiny lightbulb
    – he runs it backwards as fast as it will go and it creates the
    tiniest light you've ever seen.*

AMY (*underwhelmed*). Oh.

JOSS. Bigger the motor, stronger the light – obviously. Just the
    two of you in here?

AMY. Yes.

JOSS. Seems a shame. Pretty girl like you.

MAY. I don't think we have any motors, I'm not sure we can
    help you.

JOSS (*to* AMY). You look – familiar.

> AMY *walks towards him – slowly – looks into his face, it's as if she might kiss him – but she stops – touches his face to make sure he's real.*

AMY. I thought you might not be real.

JOSS. What a daft thing to say.

AMY. Would you like to stay for dinner?

JOSS. You ain't got no power.

AMY. No but, I could make something. I could – we could burn something – we could – have you got a lighter? We could make a fire, somehow. You could show me how, I bet you can make a fire. There are trees – in the garden, we could dig through the snow and /

MAY. / Let him go, Ames.

> —

JOSS. I should shoot off. Left my mother looking after the little one and it's a lot on her own.

MAY. Your mother?

JOSS. My wife's mother but /

MAY. / Your wife?

JOSS. Yes.

AMY. Oh.

> —

> How old is your little one… how old is your – um – how old is your /

JOSS. / A year and half or thereabouts – you should see her.

AMY. Her?

JOSS. It makes you feel so – (*Puts his hand on his chest.*) Just to look at her.

AMY. I'm sure.

JOSS. You not got any?

AMY. No.

JOSS. Never wanted?

AMY. Mum needs looking after.

MAY. That's not – that's not /

JOSS. / A son is a son till he gets him a wife but a daughter is a daughter the whole of her life.

AMY. Hm.

JOSS. I should set off. Before it gets too dark.

AMY. You got far to go?

JOSS. I'll make it home for bedtime. Thanks for being hospitable. I'd return the favour if you're ever in the area.

   JOSS *exits*.

   AMY *stares at the space where he has gone*.

AMY. He didn't say where.

MAY. What?

AMY. He said come by but he didn't say where.

MAY. It was a figure of speech.

   AMY *turns back to the window – and stares out. All is grey*.

   The snow comes down.

AMY. I'll get the duvets down.

   A knock at the door.

   He came back for me.

MAY. Don't open it. Amy.

   AMY *opens the door*.

   FAN WANG *enters*, *carrying a briefcase*.

FAN. Singer 太太, Singer 小姐 你們好，很高興認識你們。我的名字叫黃芬。
我是代表 Nangto 公司而來的。請問可否給我一點點時間？

(*Singer tàitài, Singer xiǎojiě nǐmen hǎo, hěn gāoxìng rènshí
nǐmen. Wǒ de míngzì jiào huáng fēn. Wǒ shì dàibiǎo nangto
gōngsī ér lái de. Qǐngwèn kěfǒu gěi wǒ yī diǎndiǎn shíjiān?*)
[Good evening, Mrs and Miss Singer, it's lovely to meet you
– my name is Miss Fan Wang. I am here on behalf of the
Nangto corporation, I wonder if I could ask for a little of
your time?]

AMY *and* MAY *look at each other totally nonplussed.*

我們之前发过 email 你們！ (*Wǒmen zhīqián fǎguò email gěi
nǐmen!*) [We emailed ahead to all of the homes in the
catchment area to explain that we would be popping in this
evening for a short conversation.]

AMY. I'm sorry, we don't understand you.

MAY. What do you want?

AMY. Mum.

MAY. Would you like a cup of tea?

AMY. The kettle isn't working.

FAN. 你們兩個都不會說普通話嗎？ (*Nǐmen liǎng gè dōu bù huì shuō
pǔtōnghuà ma?*) [Neither of you speak any Mandarin?]

MAY. We don't understand, I'm sorry.

FAN. 一点点也不可以嗎？ (*Yī diǎndiǎn yě bù kěyǐ ma?*) [None at
all?]

AMY. 说名字一点点 (*Shuō míngzì Yī diǎndiǎn*) [Speak just
almost my name small.]

FAN *smiles kindly at the two women.*

FAN (*to* AMY – *slow and loud as if she's stupid.*)
我是代表 Nangto 給你們看我們的 demonstration 而來的。(*Wǒ shì
dàibiǎo nangto gěi nǐmen kàn wǒmen de demonstration ér
lái de.*) [I – AM – HERE – ON BEHALF OF NANGTO. I'D
– LIKE – TO – SHOW – YOU – A – DEMONSTRATION.]

FAN *sighs, it's been a long day – she clicks in the box and we watch as it rises into the air –* AMY *is immediately entranced by it.*

這個是 Toroid (*Zhège shì toroid*) [This is the Toroid.]

AMY. 什么 Toroid 是? (*Shénme Toroid shì?*) [What Toroid is?]

FAN *smiles at* AMY.

That's right. I know that's right.

FAN. 簡單的普通話也不行? (*jiǎndān de pǔtōnghuà yě bùxíng?*) [You don't speak any Mandarin? Any at all?]

MAY. What's she saying?

AMY. She's asking why we don't speak any Mandarin. (*To* FAN.) We speak English at home – Mum doesn't speak any Mandarin. They use Mandarin at the office but I've been working from home so long, I /

/ FAN *can't understand it, annoyed, tired – decides to use her glasses to translate.*

MAY. It's a Sunday night, Miss Wang, and I'm afraid it's family time and we weren't expecting visitors and I'd appreciate it if /

FAN. / Good evening, Mrs and Miss Singer, it's lovely to meet you – my name is Miss Fan Wang, I'm here on behalf of the Nangto Corporation.

AMY. Your glasses, they're live translating?

AMY *tries to look behind the glasses for a second – she puts them on.*

這真他媽的太棒了！媽，我會說普通話了 (*zhè zhēn tā mā de tài bàngle! Mā, wǒ huì shuō pǔtōnghuà le*) [This is so fucking cool – look, Mum, I can speak Mandarin – no problem.]

FAN *laughs – takes the glasses back.*

FAN. We should stick to English, for your mum.

MAY. We don't want to buy anything, thank you.

AMY *tries to touch them as if they are magic –* FAN *smiles –
the women like each other.*

FAN. You run off a solar-panel field in the back and on the roof
and you have a central turbine field that serves all the local
holdings? You can get emergency supply from a hydrogen
cell in Penzance?

AMY. It's expensive.

MAY. We look after our own needs, thank you.

FAN. Your monthly power bills are coming in at just over
a thousand pounds?

MAY. How do you know that?

FAN. And this is your third black patch in three weeks?

AMY. It's the snow. You would have thought this country
would have learnt to deal with a bit of snow by now.

FAN *presses a button on the Toroid – it produces a low hum
– a soft light.*

MAY. You can't use our hub.

FAN. Calm down, Mrs Singer.

MAY. Don't do that, Amy, stand back.

FAN. Please. I'm trying to help you.

FAN *sets the Toroid into action – the device glows intensely –
suddenly power fills the room – the lights, the kettle, the oven,
music comes on – everything bursts into an intense – warm –
glow – it's joyous – it lets out the most incredible light.*

You can control it, obviously – I'm just indulging in a little –
circus.

AMY *can't contain herself – it's glorious – she's spellbound.*
MAY *can't take her eyes off her daughter.*

AMY. It looks like – sunshine.

AMY *reaches out to touch it.*

MAY. Careful. Come away.

FAN. It's okay.

> AMY *smiles softly* – MAY *looks at the wonder in her daughter's face – a look she hasn't seen for years.*

MAY. Love?

FAN. 這個 Toroid, 你只要一次付款 對不起！對不起！等一下 (*Zhège Toroid, nǐ zhǐyào yīcì fùkuǎn duìbùqǐ! Duìbùqǐ! Děng yīxià*) [With the Toroid – for a one-off hardware payment and a monthly supply of fuel cartridges – sorry the presentation is pre-recorded, one minute!] With the Toroid for a one-off hardware payment and a monthly supply of fuel cartridges /

AMY. / Cartridges?

FAN. The Toroid allows you to operate entirely off-grid. Independent control of your own supply. It will satisfy all your needs – full household hub appliances – scratch-make systems, entertainment surrounds and screens, car charging, self-clean, all comms and printing systems.

AMY. Everything is so much – brighter.

FAN. And faster. No more black patches. No more emergency-supply surge charges.

> AMY *stands back and stares, tries to figure it out.*

AMY. What is it? It's not connected to anything; it's generating right here. Is it…?

FAN. Cold fusion.

AMY. There's a nuclear reaction happening, there? Right – there?

FAN. You're looking at it like it's magic.

AMY. I used to sit in the university café, with my friend – and neither of us knew what we were talking about but we'd – (*Gets tearful.*) we'd draw ideas and imagine that one day – sorry – sorry – I'm – God, look at it. We dreamed of this. We thought we were so clever. We never imagined it would – I want to tell Ishbel McFarlane that they've done it, someone has done it – I don't even know where she lives any more.

FAN. We have done it, Nangto.

AMY. Yes.

MAY. It's expensive, I guess.

FAN. Three times more power than you have at the moment –
for half the price. No black patches. No surge pricing.

–

MAY *realises what this means*.

AMY. Mum?

MAY *turns away*.

FAN. I can set you up on a payment plan here and now and
leave you operational.

MAY. What happens when we need new cartridges?

FAN. Automatically ordered and delivered.

MAY. If it breaks?

FAN. Software updates respond instantly to error reports and
hardware is collected and replaced inside an hour.

MAY. Our whole life becomes reliant on a bit of stuff that only
you know how to fix – you can shut it down from the other
side of the world at a moment's notice. We all remember
Hinckley, Miss Wang.

FAN. That was long before I was born.

AMY. Mum?

MAY. They'd have us by the short and curlies and they'd make
sure we knew it.

FAN. Your current energy supplier has you sitting in the dark.

MAY. An English company.

FAN. Mrs Singer. Nangto has brought huge regeneration to this
area – the Toroid is just one more step toward /

MAY. / The Nangto factories in Penzance pay nothing and work
their employees like dogs.

FAN. Our English employees are earning a lot more than they were sitting on street corners. We pay in Yuan which is worth twice as much as the pound, we offer training schemes and free language courses – (*To* AMY.) which I can happily enrol you on. We believe that if we have the chance to educate you – we owe it to you to do so.

AMY. It's clean and safe and cheap and look, we're warm and up and running for the first time in /

MAY. / Shut it down, it's hurting my eyes.

AMY. We need it.

MAY. Where's your patriotism? Where's your self-respect?

AMY. Oh for fuck's sake.

–

FAN *looks from one woman to the other, senses the tension.*

FAN. We targeted your household in particular because of your interest in home care.

MAY. Home care?

FAN. You sent an email to our sister company asking for more information about the automated assist home-care programme?

MAY. No I didn't.

AMY. I did.

MAY. What?

FAN. With the Toriod you can run a robotic care system affordably.

MAY. Care robots?

FAN. They have intuitive intimacy programming, interchangeable soft pads and articulated limbs. I run the programme for my mother whilst I am away travelling. For an only child it is a way to achieve freedom without 'difficult feelings'. (*Touches her glasses.*) Is that the right translation?

MAY. It'll do.

FAN. Have you ever been to Beijing, Miss Singer?

AMY. No.

MAY. Miss Wang, we're done here. If you'll excuse us – we have things to be getting on with.

FAN *starts shutting the Toroid down. The lights go out – the room feels twice as dead as it did in the first place.* AMY *stares at* FAN *putting it away.*

FAN. I'll be in the area until tomorrow morning. I've sent you my card. Please do get in touch if you change your mind.

MAY. Thank you for your time.

FAN. No, no – thank you.

FAN *pops a small capsule out of the machine and puts it in her bag.*

AMY. What's that?

FAN (*the capsule*). It's the reaction's waste capsule.

AMY. What's in it?

FAN (*breathes in from the capsule*). Helium and a little deuterium, which is just heavy water.

AMY. Helium? Wait – so the fusion fuel is –

FAN. Helium 3.

AMY. But Helium 3 doesn't occur on earth, doesn't it? I thought it got burnt off by our atmosphere?

FAN. We harvest it from the Moon.

FAN *casually puts the Toroid away.*

AMY. What?

MAY. You can't do that.

FAN. The programme was started in the twenties.

AMY. We would know, we would have been told, people would know.

FAN. We've sold millions of these in China.

AMY. Why don't we know?

MAY. You can't own the moon.

FAN. We have been granted a thousand-year concession by the Global Union.

AMY. No one can own the Moon. No one can give permission for /

FAN. / No one owned the Earth until people arrived and said they did. Ladies, I must /

MAY. / The Moon is not Chinese.

FAN. We have Saudi Arabian and Russian shareholders in the project – so don't worry, we won't be turning it red just yet.

FAN *laughs a little – it's kindly – she's joking with them.*

MAY. It's dangerous.

FAN. No. Not at all.

MAY. I – I – the tides.

FAN. If we harvested one thousand tons of lunar soil a day it would take two hundred and twenty billion years to decrease the mass of the moon by nought-point-one per cent. It would never effect the tides.

AMY. There will be dangers. Of course there will.

FAN. None that we know of. I'm afraid I have appointments with your neighbours that I must keep. (*Shakes* AMY*'s hand.*) You should come to Beijing some day. I think you would like it. Good evening, ladies.

FAN *exits – takes the Toroid with her.*

–

MAY. Bloody cheek, sales calls on a Sunday night. It shouldn't be allowed.

–

AMY. I'll get the duvets down.

MAY. Not on my account, love.

AMY. Well you can't get them on your own and it's the only way to get warm, so.

The two women stare at each other for some time – stand-off.

MAY. I used to come home at eight or nine after a full day's work. My knees would go out from under me. I'd relieve a surly childminder; I'd cook a proper meal, hardly able to keep my eyes open and then I'd sit and talk to you – for an hour, two hours about your day. Which place did you get in the running race? Always making sure I remembered what place you'd come the week before. How was the situation with Jacinta? Had she stolen your ruler again? I'd bath you, I'd read you a story, I'd kiss you goodnight and you'd sleep soundly, so soundly. I'd watch you and then I'd have to drag myself away and work for another two, three hours – then in the early hours of the morning, the silence – the exhaustion, the loneliness would hit me like a fucking tidal wave. I'd crawl to the bathroom because it was furthest away from your room, lock the door, put a towel across the crack at the bottom to muffle the sound and I would howl – on my hands and knees I would howl – as silently as I could, sob as noiselessly as I could. Most nights I'd end up sleeping on the bathroom floor – until 5 a.m. came and the alarm went and I'd have to find a suit without food on it and make breakfast and do it all over again. That is what I held. That is what I swallowed. That is what I protected you from.

AMY. You forgot the bit about the car.

MAY. What?

AMY. Usually when you tell that story you start with sitting in the car not sure that you have the strength to walk through the front door. It's usually before the childminder bit.

MAY *stares at* AMY.

MAY *slaps* AMY.

The women stare.

Why did you leave him?

MAY. So we could be free.

*Suddenly in a house just across the way – we see the light
of the Toroid – flash – bright in the night sky –* AMY *can't
take her eyes off it – she stares and stares at the light, she's
transfixed by it –* MAY *stares at her daughter. In the flash
of the Toroid –* MA SINGER *– is suddenly sitting at the
kitchen table. She looks at* MAY *– they hold one another's
eye.* AMY *can't take her eyes off the Toroid – she stands in
the doorway.*

Put your arms around me.

AMY. If you get warm you'll be colder than you started five
minutes after.

MAY. Then keep your arms around me.

AMY. I might go out for a walk or I won't sleep.

MAY. Walk? You'll freeze.

AMY. Just a minute or two – see the size of the sky.

MAY. I love you. That's all.

AMY. I love you too. Very very much.

AMY *walks toward the door – stares out.*

Mum?

MAY. Hm.

AMY. Thank you.

AMY *exits.*

MAY *sits. Time passes.*

Footsteps – someone is at the door – MAY *gets up,
desperate to see who it is – we've never seen her move so
fast – desperate for it to be* AMY.

MAY. Love? Love – Amy – love, it's me – it's Mum – love?

MAY *opens the door – it's not* AMY.

MAY *stands*.

WILLIAM WHITCOMB *enters – he looks at* MAY. *Music
plays.* MAY *and* WW *line dance to Justin Bieber. He takes
a bottle of brandy out of his saddlebag and gives* MAY *a
glass – he laughs. His lamp throws soft light across the
room. He takes* MAY, *he spins her round – they waltz. The
light throws their shadows up large across the walls. Two
ageing survivors dance and dance – like gods, like monsters.*

WW. You ever think we were born at exactly the right moment?
That you got to see exactly the right bit – right at the top of
things?

WW *steps back and looks at* MAY*'s face*.

There's something about you.

The light of the Toroid zings out in the distance.

The age of oil now comes to a close.

Interscene

MAY *and* WW *freeze, as if stuck in time; snow globe, museum exhibit.* FAN WANG *puts a coin into the machine and brings the historical exhibit to life – she stares at it, barely interested. Her phone rings – she answers it and chats over the top of:*

EXHIBIT RECORDING.

suí zhe néng yuán shí dài de zhōng jié   xī fāng dì guó yě cóng
随 着 能 源 时 代 的 终 结， 西 方 帝 国 也 从

ér zǒu xiàng shuāi luò   hé yǐ qián céng jīng chū xiàn guò de
而 走 向 衰 落。和 以 前 曾 经 出 现 过 的

luó mǎ dì guó yí yàng   zhè ge xī fāng dì guó yě zì yǐ wéi tā
罗 马 帝 国 一 样， 这 个 西 方 帝 国 也 自 以 为 他

men de xiàn dài mó shì   biàn shì wú kě qǔ dài de xiàn dài huà
们 的 现 代 模 式， 便 是 无 可 取 代 的 现 代 化

běn shēn
本 身。

[As the Age of Oil came to a close so this Western Empire fell into decline. The Western Empire, like the Roman Empire that had come before, made the false assumption that their version of modernity was modernity itself.]

The announcement then repeats in computerised English.

FAN WANG *is disinterested – she has other things to do – she exits.*

AMY. I keep thinking what if all this time, I've seen control and manipulation and actually it was just love.

So much – love. Endless, infinite – and I just couldn't.

–

And it's going to be gone.

And I won't be able to get it back.

And when it is – I think it's going to be the kind of regret that…

Fade to black.

Other Titles in this Series

www.nickhernbooks.co.uk

facebook.com/nickhernbooks

twitter.com/nickhernbooks

ELLA HICKSON

Ella Hickson is an award-winning writer whose work has been
performed throughout the UK and abroad. In 2013–14 *Wendy
& Peter Pan* played to wide acclaim at the Royal Shakespeare
Company. Other credits include *Riot Girls* (Radio 4), *Boys*
(Nuffield Theatre, Southampton/Headlong Theatre/HighTide
Festival Theatre), *Decade* (Headlong Theatre/St Katherine's
Dock), *The Authorised Kate Bane* (Grid Iron/Traverse Theatre),
Rightfully Mine (Radio 4), *Precious Little Talent* (Trafalgar
Studios/Tantrums Productions), *Hot Mess* (Arcola Tent/
Tantrums Productions) and *Eight* (Trafalgar Studios/Bedlam
Theatre, Edinburgh). In 2011 Ella was the Pearson writer-in-
residence at the Lyric Theatre Hammersmith and she is the
recipient of the 2013 Catherine Johnson Award.

Her short film *Hold On Me* premiered at the 55th BFI London
Film Festival. Ella is writing new plays for the National Theatre
and the Royal Shakespeare Company.